The Beauty of Pain

Noor Niami

THE BEAUTY OF PAIN

Copyright © 2020 by Noor Niami

Published by: Noor Niami

For information contact:

Noor Niami

www.noorniami.com

Second Printing, 2020

ISBN: 978-0-6489327-0-3 (paperback)

"Behind every beautiful thing, there's been some kind of pain."

Bob Dylan

Dedicated to you

Don't wait for the light at the end of the tunnel, become the light you need instead.

This is my intention for you and for the world.

Contents

Acknowledgement

When I first sat down to write a book, I knew it was the right thing to do at the right time. I tried writing before that but would stop halfway because I wasn't ready. I was still going through my healing and wasn't ready to write about something I haven't accomplished. But now I was ready, more than ever before, and I was determined to share the hope, the joy, the life I experienced after embracing my pain and healing myself back to wholeness. Fast forward to now and here you are holding the creation of a new book in your hands.

First and foremost, I would like to acknowledge God and my Lord and Savior, Jesus Christ. My redemption, healing and restoration wouldn't have been possible if it wasn't for the love and mercy of God through Jesus Christ. When the world rejected me, God accepted me. When the world broke me, God healed me. And when the world hated me, God loved me. God turned that little broken girl into a woman of truth, power, and wisdom. I am a living example that God turns broken things into beautiful things and He turned my brokenness into beauty, my pain into power. None of this would've been possible if it wasn't for His unfailing love, grace and mercy so I give all the glory to God.

The Lord is my strength and my shield, my heart trusts in Him.

Secondly, I wouldn't have gotten through the darkest times of my life if it wasn't for my beautiful parents. They saw me at my absolute worst and darkest times. They helped me in ways I can't describe and I don't know where I'd be today if it wasn't for them.

And to my mum, Hana; I wouldn't be the woman I am today without your unconditional, unlimited love and kindness. You gave me strength when I was weak, you gave me hope when I was hopeless, and you gave me courage when I was afraid. You lifted me up every time I fell and you loved me even when I was hard to love. You never gave up on me and always believed in me even when I couldn't believe in myself. You helped me become the woman I am today and no matter what I do I'll never be able to repay you for everything you've done for me. You are my strength, my joy, and my blessing sent from above.

So to you mum and dad, I love you more than words can describe and I thank you for being by my side every step of the way. You are the light and the love of my heart.

Introduction

The Beauty of Pain is a collection of reflections on life through the eyes of a human who has experienced most of life in pain, fear, and heartbreak. It is written in the words of a person who came from a place of utter despair and brokenness to complete healing and wholeness. It is written in the voice of every person who has been hurt, betrayed, abandoned, misjudged and mistreated. But also in the voice of every person who didn't give up even when giving up seemed easier.

Beauty begins the moment we embrace our pain. We spend so many years running away from our pain and recoil in fear the moment it starts to get uncomfortable, but by doing so we let our pain dig its roots deeper, grow bigger, and live longer. It will continue to do so for as long as we run and leave it unattended.

Pain has a purpose; pain is there to show you what you need to address. Don't turn away but embrace it, sit and be with it. The very act of recognising and accepting your pain will allow it to serve its purpose. You will later discover the beauty and the power of pain. The darkness you're in today will lead you into the light and your biggest pain will turn into your greatest gain.

The Beauty of Pain doesn't just belong to me; it belongs to everyone whose path has crossed mine. Our journey in life may be different but I believe the pain we experience as humans is that of the same; feeling of hopelessness, despair, and confusion to name a few. Nonetheless, had my journey not have been what it was, with every story and every detail, I would not be the person I am today.

My intention for this book is to bring you light, hope, and power. To help you transcend your level of thinking to a higher level of truth and perspective. To turn you from a victim of your circumstances into a victorious warrior, overcoming every storm and climbing every mountain.

May this book give a voice to those who need one, be a light in someone's darkness, bring hope into what might seem like a hopeless situation and inspire those who need a reminder of the power they have over their lives.

Remember, it's not about the words that are in this book, it's about what you make of them.

And I promise you from the bottom of my heart, from someone who's been through what you're going through; the pain that you've been feeling now can't compare to the joy that's coming.

With love & light,

You Needed to Be Broken

Until you're broken, you don't know what you're made out of. Our brokenness gives us the opportunity to build ourselves all over again, but stronger than ever before. To be reborn, you must die first and when you're broken, the only way to get back up is to rebuild yourself. Do not fight the pain; embrace it. Accept it. Feel it. Live it. Allow your brokenness to be turned into beauty and your pain into glory because at the loss of something you will in fact gain something greater and your biggest lessons will turn into your biggest blessings. And this is the beauty of pain.

– Noor Niami

You Are Worthy

You are worthy beyond measure, I cannot put it in enough words to describe the measure of your worth but you need to know to the deepest core of your being that you are absolutely worthy. You are worthy regardless of what anyone else says, does, or thinks. Because it isn't about anyone else, it's about you knowing your own self-worth. You don't seek your self-worth and value from outside forces because your worth and value must be known and lived from within. It is a truth you must embody and live regardless of what is happening on the outside of you. You cannot see yourself through the eyes of someone else and you shouldn't be asking them to value your worth because you will always be selling yourself short. People can only see you from their level of understanding and awareness so don't let someone who doesn't know your value tell you how much you're worth. You need to see your worth through your lenses and if your lenses are distorted then you have the power to change the way you see yourself. You were fearfully and wonderfully made and everything you will ever need already exists within you. And it is our responsibility and purpose to find the treasure that already lies within. You are pure love and joy and worthy beyond measure. But you must believe this first otherwise nothing else will matter because you will only believe what you have told yourself. Remember that your worth and value does not decrease based on someone's inability to see your worth, it only decreases based on your inability to see your worth. There will always be someone who can't see your worth, don't let it be you.

– Noor Niami

It Doesn't Matter Where You Came From

It doesn't matter where you came from, what matters is where you're going. We've all been in places we didn't want to be in and done things we're not proud of and weren't our finest moments, but isn't it through these moments we've learned our greatest lessons? So why regret anything in the past when everything up until now has made you into the person you are today leading you to where you're going? Do not regret your past; no matter how shameful or unpleasant it was because you were doing the best of what you knew then. Don't say to yourself I wish I knew then what I know now because what you know now is a result of what you didn't know then. So in essence everything you have been through is preparing you to where you're going and you're doing the best of what you can in every moment and that is enough. Go easy on yourself, be gentle and have patience. Everyone has had a past but it's what you choose to do with it that will set you apart from the rest. You can dwell there for as long as you want and not get anywhere, or you can let it go knowing that you are not your past and one bad chapter isn't the end of your story. Turn your pain into gain and let your past be a stepping stone to your future, which will be better than anything you have ever imagined.

– Noor Niami

You Are Becoming

You are strong because you've been weak.

You are fearless because you've been afraid.

You are wise because you've been foolish.

You are bold because you've been timid.

You are powerful because you've been powerless.

You have become who you truly are as a result of once being who you are not. So everything you have been through has led you back to yourself and everything you've endured has made you into who you are today. Nothing is ever wasted and everything is happening *for* you, to bring you to your highest good and greatest joy.

– Noor Niami

Forgiveness

Don't allow yourself to harbor resentment and bitterness towards those who have hurt you. It sucks to be hurt, especially by those closest to us, but it happens to everybody and just like we've been hurt we've also hurt others. Here's the thing, most people are unconscious and their level of awareness is slim to none so they themselves don't even understand what they're doing or why they're doing it. And if we're honest with ourselves, then we will admit that we were once just like them. We were living life from the outside in and doing things unconsciously because we were asleep like the rest. It takes a lot of effort to be woke in an asleep world and stay woke amongst people who are asleep. Not many people will go through your kind of growth to get to your level of awareness because growth is painful and few find the courage to go through the pain in order to grow and evolve. Another very important truth to consider when forgiving those who have hurt you is this; the pain they have inflicted on you must have come from somewhere, it didn't just pop out of the air. Do you know from where? The pain came from *them*; it had to travel *to* them first to get through to you. Because we are all vessels of something and it's up to us to choose what we hold inside of us. This is why we say hurting people hurt people because if you are well and happy you don't go around hurting people, for love and pain cannot abide in the same heart. It's not possible. Forgive them knowing that for them to hurt you then they must be unwell and hurting too. And remember forgiveness isn't excusing their actions or giving them another opportunity to hurt you with; forgiveness is about setting yourself free because you deserve peace and freedom.

– Noor Niami

You Are Where You Need to Be

Don't despise where you're at because you are exactly where you need to be in this moment, right here right now. Fighting against it will only make it worse and the longer you fight it the longer you'll be stuck in the same place because what you give attention to grows. The key is to surrender and accept what is and make peace with where you are. What you give power to has power over you. So if you're fighting with your circumstances and wishing they were different you're in fact creating more of what is because your attention is drawn to it. Have you ever wondered why you seem to be getting more of the same? Where attention goes energy flows, so you need to take your attention off it, make peace with it and accept it for what it is, don't try to make it into what it's not. It is what it is and when you accept it you stop the struggle and find peace. Then you can start enjoying the journey rather than worry so much about the destination. Sooner or later you will reach your destination but you decide how you get there. You can have a joyful or a miserable journey, the choice is yours. Often we think we need the place to change but it is our attitude towards it that needs changing and when we change our attitude we change our perspective and change our life. Take off the conditions and live your life unconditionally. Living a conditional life will make you a prisoner of your own mind but living an unconditional life is freedom, joy, and happiness. I don't know about you but I know which one I would choose.

– Noor Niami

Replace Fear With Faith

In every situation and in all circumstances let your faith be bigger than your fear. Faith and fear both require you to believe in something you cannot see. Choose faith over fear, choose faith over doubt, choose faith over the unknown, for where faith is there is your power too. Faith is the confidence that what we hope for will actually happen and fear is the confidence that it will not, both give us the assurance about things which we cannot see. It's okay to be afraid but it's harder to always live in fear. Choose faith to live life rather than fear life. Faith is seeing light with your heart when all your eyes can see is darkness. No matter how bad your circumstances are, there's always hope if you have faith. All things are possible to him who believes. Faith is the power you have to create your life; create what you love, not what you fear.

– Noor Niami

You Are Not a Victim

You are anything but a victim; you are a victorious warrior and a fighter. When you see yourself as a victim you shred yourself of your power completely leaving you feeling powerless and hopeless. Self-pity and victimisation of oneself is the worst thing you can ever do to yourself. It is an awful emotion to feel and it diminishes you to literally nothing. You will be left feeling depleted and depressed and you cannot get anywhere from that state of being. Self-pity comes with a heavy price, the consequences are severe and you need to try your best to take yourself out of that state. You are not a product of your circumstances, you are not your mistakes and you need to stand up high knowing that you still hold the power and, you can and will overcome the giant standing in front of you. The battle is there to be won but you cannot have a winner's attitude with a victim's mentality. You need to see yourself as a victorious warrior, a fighter and a winner and your actions will follow through and you will face and defeat those demons standing in front of you. You are more than capable and able to overcome anything that comes at you. The thing you thought was sent for your destruction will be used for your construction and what was meant to break you will make you. You might stumble and fall and that is okay, it doesn't matter how many times you fall, what matters is whether or not you choose to get up. Remember the lower the fall the higher the rise, you need to fall to the lowest lows to get to the highest highs.

– Noor Niami

Phoenix Rising

And just as the Phoenix rose from the ashes, you too will rise from yours. You will conquer demons and win battles no one knows anything about. You will wear your scars like wings and just like that you will learn how to fly and rise above what was meant to bury you. You will become the fire that once tried to consume you; returning from the flames, clothed in nothing but honour, strength, and power.

– Noor Niami

One of a Kind

You are one of a kind and there is no one else like you in this world and there is your power. You are special and unique and this sets you apart from anyone else. Don't compare yourself with anybody else because there is no comparison between the sun and the moon, they both shine when it's their time. Don't change who you are to be someone you are not but accept and embrace yourself as you are. You don't need to be accepted by others, you just need to be accepted by yourself and when you accept yourself then the whole world will accept you too. We are all a work in progress and what you were yesterday is not who you are today or who you will be tomorrow. You are constantly changing and evolving into your highest level of expression and when you accept that you are not perfect then you can learn to accept your flaws and forgive yourself. Accept yourself as you are and only then will you cease being someone you're not. Be strong, be beautiful and be confident by just being you.

– Noor Niami

Don't Dim Your Light

Don't dim your light because it's shining in their eyes. Don't dim your light because it's showing them their darkness. That's not your cross to carry or your problem to bear. Shining your light makes them see themselves for who they really are, and they don't want to see something they don't like. Don't be offended if they reject you and don't want you around them, it's not personal. The spirit in you irritates the demons in them. Don't dim your light but shine brighter than ever before. Everyone wants to be the sun but to be the sun you need to first burn like the sun.

– Noor Niami

Rejection is a Redirection

Rejection is a redirection to something bigger and better. It's easy to be dismayed and discouraged when people reject us. It hurts when the people you love the most are the ones who reject you the most but what if I told you even their rejection is part of the plan on your life? What if I said they have done exactly what they were supposed to do and their God-given purpose was in fact to reject you? Would you believe me? Because this is the highest form of truth, you may not be ready to accept it yet and that's okay, give yourself time to heal because rejection hurts. But later on you will realise this was actually a blessing in disguise. There were many blessings hidden in their rejection, some you will see now and some will be revealed to you at the right time. But ultimately their rejection will be used as a redirection to put you on a different path than the one you were on. And this path will take you to a far better destination than the path you were on before. Their rejection will also birth you in your self-acceptance and had they not rejected you, you wouldn't have learned how to love and accept yourself. And when you love yourself you will never ever rely on anyone else to validate you because you have learned to validate and accept yourself from within and this is ultimate freedom. Their rejection led you back to yourself; to accept and embrace yourself fully and completely.

– Noor Niami

To Be Reborn, You Must Die First

Everything that has happened to you has actually been happening *for* you. You were meant to be broken so that you could die, not a literal death but a spiritual death of self. The old you has to die at some point in your life because you can no longer think, act, or live life the way you have been. The old you, dictated by your ego, has now become detrimental to your soul and wellbeing so a destruction of the ego must now take place. Our ego is not who we are, so we need to die of who we are not in order to become who we truly are. It's only when we are broken down, light can then enter through the cracks and heal us and this is why it is said when we are weak then are we strong because light, grace, and power will enter you through the cracks. And the cracks wouldn't have been there if you weren't broken first. You have to die on the inside to be reborn and you will rise from the ashes that were meant to bury you. You will rise into your true authentic self; embodied in truth, strength, power, and wisdom.

– Noor Niami

Don't Go Back

The person who broke you can't be the one to fix you so stop looking for happiness in the same place you lost it. Don't go back to something God had to rescue you from. You cannot heal in the same environment that made you sick and you cannot grow in the same soil that poisoned you.

— Noor Niami

Embrace Your Pain

Embrace your pain and don't run from it. From a very young age we've all been taught to hide and bury our 'bad' feelings because they're a sign of weakness and you don't want to be a weak person amongst strong people right? But this isn't right nor is it true. The ones who hide their pain and pretend to be strong are in fact weak and the ones who embrace their pain and show their vulnerability are in fact strong. Because pain requires courage; and vulnerability requires honesty, and both are attributes of great strength. But instead of embracing our pain we spend all our lives running away from it. But the truth of the matter is; nothing ever goes away until we face it. Nothing at all. And here's the thing; the fear of your pain is more painful than the pain itself. It is your fear of it that makes it so much worse than what it actually is if you only just sit with it for a little while. Embrace it and let it teach you things you didn't know. Pain is the best teacher you'll ever have because it'll teach you things you've never been taught. The more we ignore our pain the bigger our pain will get and this is why things get worse before they get better. What we need to do is stop running and start facing, and you do this by going from within because the battle is within you. You need to embrace all of your feelings, sit with them, acknowledge them, feel them, and accept them as a part of you. Then bless them and release them. It's important to also know this isn't an overnight job so being patient with yourself is going to be a must. Being kind to yourself in the process is also a must because facing our own demons requires a lot of courage and strength. Both of which you cannot have if you are not patient and kind to yourself first. And I am here to promise you with all my heart that your greatest pain will turn into your greatest gain in so many ways if you just keep going and never give up.

– Noor Niami

Finding You

Letting go of someone you love romantically will be one of the hardest things you will ever do because your soul is going to be so enmeshed with theirs that the two of you had become one. So when you're letting them go you'll also be letting a part of yourself go with them, a part of you that you will never get back. But you must let them go to hold on to what's left of you because holding on to them is making you lose yourself. You must let them go to find you because somewhere along the journey you lost yourself. You held on to them at the expense of losing yourself so now you must lose them to find yourself. Then you will realise by losing them, you found you so you haven't lost at all, you won. You will then realise you are the person you have been looking for all your life and you had to let them go in order to find you.

– Noor Niami

Be True to Yourself

Always be you. Never be anyone else but you because it takes a lot of energy trying to be someone you're not. Don't let a dark world dim your light and don't let the poor actions of others define who you are. Don't change yourself to please others or to seek their approval but only change to become a better version of you for yourself. The second you start doing it for someone else then you've stopped being true to yourself and no one is worth you losing yourself over. Somebody's poor actions and words are not in any way a reflection of you but a reflection of who they are. For out of the treasure of the heart the mouth speaks and you shall know them by their fruit. If your inside is rotten you will bring forth rotten things, but if your inside is beautiful you will bring forth beautiful things, so don't let their rottenness damage your beauty because you are beautiful just the way you are. Stay true to yourself so those who matter can be true to you.

– Noor Niami

The Relationship With Yourself

You must love yourself first before anyone else can love you. We go looking and searching for love in all the wrong places. We look for the ideal partner, the one who can grant us the love and approval that we are unable to grant ourselves. But you can't get there from there, it won't work. Because the world outside of you is a mirror of the world inside of you. How you feel about yourself on the inside will be reflected by someone else on the outside. If you don't love and value yourself then you will be with someone who will not love and value you because they are a perfect match to what you've got going on, on the inside. Your relationship with them will be the reflection of your relationship with yourself. They are mirroring back to you how you feel about yourself. This is how you called them into your life in the first place. Can you now see the power you hold over your life? Once you change the relationship you have with yourself, the one with your inner being, then life and others will start to mirror back to you exactly that, nothing more and nothing less. The love that you are now emanating from within will come back to you through people and experiences reflecting to you the love you already hold for yourself. And anyone who does not match your now reality from within will fall off your experience and new ones will emerge but it all starts and ends with you. As above, so below, as within, so without.

– Noor Niami

Start Again

Don't be afraid to start all over again, you won't be starting from scratch. This time around you will be starting from a far better place than the place you originally started from, you are starting from experience. You are not the same person you used to be, and what you know now you didn't know back then so you are fully loaded with everything you now need to succeed in starting all over again. You're stronger and wiser now to begin again and succeed. Believe in yourself, start again, keep trying and never give up on yourself and you will see how the things you deemed as failures were actually part of your plan to succeed, everything has equipped and empowered you for what you are about to do now. You don't have to see the full road ahead just start by taking the first step.

– Noor Niami

You Intimidate Them

The people who belittle you, put you down, and find faults in you are the ones who are intimated by you the most. They don't mind seeing you do well but they never want to see you do better than them and do something they're not doing. They don't want you having something they can't have because they're not willing to do what you've done. Your success will shine on their failure so they start to diminish and devalue you because the only way they can feel better about themselves is by putting you down. But remember whoever is trying to bring you down is already below you. They want to bring you down to where they are so they can feel somewhat better that they're not alone in their misery. Don't accept their invite to their pity-party but kindly refuse and go about doing you. If they get offended then that's not your problem unless you make it yours so don't feed into their negativity. Stay in your high place and don't lower yourself to meet them, let them come up to meet you if they want to.

– Noor Niami

Endings And Beginnings

Endings bring new beginnings but between every ending and beginning there is an in-between place, a transition period. Everyone says endings bring new beginnings but when you don't see a sign of your new beginning anywhere you get discouraged and confused because no one tells you that after every ending and before any beginning there is another place you need to get to first. There is an in-between place also referred to as the wilderness in biblical terms that you must travel to first in order to cross from one side to the other. It's not in the ending or beginning that your biggest battles and greatest victories will be won, but it is in the wilderness that you will fight your greatest battles and learn your biggest lessons. So whenever something ends don't expect a brand new beginning straight away because there is a place you must get to first, not literal but a place your soul must travel to first. It is in this place you will need to unlearn everything you've once known and learn a new way of life and a new way of living. To cross over to the other side, you will need to go through this place, and to get to where you're going from where you are you will need to face your demons because they are what's standing between you and your blessing. To cross over to the other side you'll need to face your fears and let go of everything that's holding you back. Never give up because your new beginning awaits you and you are where you need to be to get to where you want to be.

– Noor Niami

To The One I Loved

I held on to you for so long, much longer than needed and much longer than anyone else would have held on to you. I forgot who I was by trying to be who you wanted me to be. I lost my self-worth and value because I was seeing myself through your eyes. I lived for you, I did everything for you. I went above and beyond and did things out of the ordinary just to make you smile and cheer you up whenever you were down. Your wish was my command, you asked, I did. Yet the more I did the less you appreciated, the more I gave, the more you expected. But on that day, something clicked within me and I was done. I was done for good this time. I've never been so sure of anything than the fact I was done and it was over. I found the courage to crush the last pieces remaining of my heart because the pain of staying with you became greater than the pain to walk away from you. My pain gave me the strength to walk away and never look back. And from thereon I promised myself I would never allow anyone else to treat me the way you treated me because my love for myself will always be greater than my love for anyone else. I will never love anyone the way I loved you and I thank God for that.

— Noor Niami

Season of Waiting

We all hate waiting and if there's one thing we lack the most is patience. In a fast-paced world with ever-changing and ever-evolving technology things are as easy and quick as they've ever been and we can literally get everything at the touch of a finger. Whilst this is a blessing, it can also be a curse because we learn to be impatient and demanding, wanting everything right now. But matters of the heart and soul take time, your dreams to come to pass will take time and to get from one place to the other requires a period of waiting. Don't despise the wait because it is in your season of waiting the most will take place. When you're waiting and thinking nothing is happening, that's when everything is actually happening behind the scenes, it is in the waiting season that we change the most. When you're in a season of waiting, it's not just a season of waiting. It's a season of preparation, sanctification, strengthening, self-improvement, tearing down, and building up. Waiting is not passive but it is very active. You are getting prepared for what you have prayed and asked for. Be patient and kind to yourself and embrace the waiting season because once you get to where you're going you will realise it was not just about the destination but about the journey and the person you have become as a result of the journey.

– Noor Niami

Those Who Hurt You Helped You

A day will come where you will look back and realise that everything was actually working out *for* you even when it didn't seem like it at the time. You will be thankful for those who hurt you and rejected you because if they hadn't tried to break you down you wouldn't have known you were unbreakable. If they didn't reject you, you wouldn't have known how to accept yourself and if they didn't cause you to fall you wouldn't have had the chance to rise. So everything that was meant to break you and crush you was used to actually make you into the stronger person you are today. The people who have hurt you and rejected you forced you into turning to yourself and learning how to love and accept yourself. If it wasn't for them hurting you, you wouldn't have learned to love yourself, if it wasn't for them rejecting you, you wouldn't have learned to accept yourself, and if it wasn't for them letting you go, you wouldn't have had the chance to find yourself. They who have hurt you have in essence blessed you by helping you find your way back home, to you.

– Noor Niami

The Best is Yet to Come

Your current circumstances are not your final destination and where you are now is leading you to where you want to be. You know you are not where you used to be, yet you are not where you want to be, but this should tell you that the best is yet to come. It may sound like a cliché but your best days are in fact ahead of you. You may have gone through a great ordeal of pain as a result of what has happened to you but remember the storm comes before the rainbow and you must go through the worst before you can get to the best. It is in your worst times you will learn the most valuable lessons, it is in the storm you will build character, perseverance, and strength. Every level will require a new version of yourself and every level brings with it a new devil so every level will require a stronger version of yourself. This is why battles are sent your way, not to defeat you, but to strengthen you and teach you how to fight and be victorious. No matter where you are at this moment know and believe in your heart that something amazing is coming your way. What's coming will far exceed your wildest dreams and expectations, all you require is a little bit of faith and patience and let things unfold for you in their perfect divine timing.

– Noor Niami

You Can't Take Everyone With You

You can't take everyone with you to where you're going. You can't climb to the top by carrying the weight of others because their weight will drag you down and this is a sure thing just as the law of gravity. You won't be able to carry them and go up, they must be willing to climb up themselves and climbing will require a lot of strength and courage and not everyone is willing to go through the journey you're on and that's okay. Not everyone will understand your journey and that's fine because it is yours to understand. Accept that everybody you came with can't go where you're going so you will need to let them go because you won't be able to take yourself to the next level by sinking to everyone else's. Let go of what is weighing you down so you can climb up to the top and once you get to the top the view will be extraordinary and worth the journey.

– Noor Niami

They May Still Love You

They may still love you, they probably do. They probably don't know what they want. They probably still think about you all the time. But that's not what matters. What matters is what are they doing about it, and what they're doing about it is nothing. And if they're doing nothing, you most certainly shouldn't do anything. You need someone who goes out of their way to make it obvious that they want you in their life. Let them go because you deserve to be with someone who is willing to fight for you. You deserve someone who will do what it takes to be with you. You deserve better, it's as simple as that.

– Noor Niami

Happiness Cannot Be Found

Happiness isn't something you can look for and find because it is something you *create*. Most people wander around wanting the same thing; true happiness. What is true happiness anyway? If you don't know what you're looking for then how are you going to find it? People think true happiness is getting what you want all the time, or it is in finding someone or having something but even if they do they are still not happy. Look at the rich and poor for example, although the rich have everything they want they are unhappy and whilst the poor have little to none they are happier. Because happiness isn't found in people or things outside of you, happiness is created on the inside. True unconditional happiness is happiness inside you. It is living in peace and harmony with yourself, your body, mind, soul, and spirit. True happiness is a state of being in love with yourself because by loving yourself unconditionally and being truly happy you neither need other people nor things. This is why we cannot search for happiness and find it because happiness is a choice we need to make, it's a decision you make that you are going to be happy without any conditions no matter what is or isn't happening outside of you. Some might aid you in getting there but your happiness ultimately comes from within. Your relationship with yourself determines the level of happiness or misery you live in, the choice is yours. Don't wait or prolong your happiness until you get somewhere or have something, but choose to be happy now without any conditions. You have the ability to be happy now regardless of outside circumstances and the irony of this is once you are happy from within yourself everything on the outside of you changes as a result of your newfound happiness.

– Noor Niami

Food For Thought

Part of the reason why we hold on to something so tight is that we fear if we let it go something great won't happen twice. But if what we had was great we wouldn't have had to let it go in the first place. Let that sink in.

– Noor Niami

Walk Away

You need to walk away from what you wanted to find what you deserve. Not everything we want is what we deserve because at first we don't even know what it is that we deserve due to our inability to see our worth. Our inability to see our self-worth makes us settle for far less than what we deserve but you need to walk away from what you wanted in order to find what you deserve. We fear the unknown but everything we want is on the other side of that fear. You need to let go of what you want to allow space for what you deserve to come in. And here's a reminder for you; you are not a backup plan, you are not someone's second choice and you are certainly not an option. You are worth more than that, you deserve better. Never settle to be someone's second best when you could be someone's best. Raise your standards and choose to wait for the person who will treat you with the same respect and consideration you would treat them. Don't accept being someone else's second option when you can be someone else's priority. Don't settle for less just because you're impatient to wait for the best.

– Noor Niami

Be Kind to Yourself

No matter what you have been through or what you are going through remember to always be kind and gentle with yourself. If it seems like the world has turned against you then the least you could do is not join them in turning against yourself. If you turn against yourself then you've just become one of them. You are worthy of the love and support you give to others freely so can you try and give some of it back to yourself? Life hits us at one stage or another and the greatest battles will be given to those of great strength. The battles are sent not to destroy us but they are sent to awaken us to the power and strength we hold within. We will make mistakes, we will fall down, we will say things and do things we're not proud of but this is how we learn. We need to go through the experience to learn the lesson so don't beat yourself up for what you didn't know before going through it. Bless every experience because it has taught you what you know and I promise you; even when it doesn't feel like it, life is always working out for you. You may not understand what is happening now but later you will. Be kind to yourself in the process and let your kindness fill the world.

– Noor Niami

Missing Them

Missing them doesn't mean you need them back. Of course you will miss them because they were a big part of your life and you will miss that part of your life from time to time. This is all just part of letting go and moving on. You let go a little then you hold on a little until you are ready to fully let go and move on. But just because you miss them it doesn't mean you need them back in your life. Sometimes it's better to close the door and accept that the past will never be the future. Stop going back to what your heart is trying to heal from, you can't heal a wound if you keep touching it.

– Noor Niami

What Doesn't Kill You

We've all heard the saying what doesn't kill you makes you stronger. But I'm here to tell you that it will certainly not kill, yes it will tear you down, but it will also build you up. It will weaken you but also make you stronger. It wasn't sent to kill you, it was sent to make you stronger and that's exactly who you'll become once you have made it through. There are going to be excruciating moments in your life, moments that you can't control and it will change your entire world in a matter of minutes and your life will never be the same again. These moments will not only change your life but they will also change you and you will never be the same person you used to be. And that's okay because the person you are becoming will cost you the person you once were. Let these moments make you stronger, wiser and kinder. But don't you let it break you and make you someone you're not. Fall down, cry and scream if you need to but eventually you will need to get up, straighten out that crown of yours and keep going. This was sent to make you stronger and it'll do just that.

– Noor Niami

Toxic People

You will come across toxic people in your life that try to control and manipulate you for their personal agenda. They will project their distorted false selves and traumas onto you and make you believe they're yours and you're the one with the problem. Don't believe in their lies and recognise who you are from them. They feed off negativity, chaos, and disorder; they point fingers and shift the blame, they refuse to take responsibility and accountability. People who are not happy with themselves cannot possibly be happy with you. Don't soak up their problems and make it your own. Quit playing with a toxic person because it is a game you will always lose. The only way to win is to not play at all.

– Noor Niami

Falling Down

It's not about falling down; it's about whether or not you get back up. It doesn't matter if you fall down because you will, we all do but what matters is whether or not we get up. Some falls will be harder than others and sometimes we'll stay down longer because the pain will be stronger, but one way or another we must find a way to get back up. Just because you've fallen down it doesn't mean you stay there and make yourself at home. You have the power to rise above whatever you've stumbled on and use it as your stepping stone to rise up. Strength isn't produced in never falling down but it is produced in rising up every time we fall. Your biggest setback will be a setup for your biggest comeback. If you lost your spark when you were down then it's okay because when you rise up, the fire in your heart will reignite and your light will shine bright. No one can stop you then because your strength will burn brighter than your fear.

– Noor Niami

Let Go And Let God

If God doesn't fix the situation then He's using the situation to fix you. God has the ability to turn your brokenness into beauty, given that you give Him all your broken pieces. He cannot heal that which you're not willing to surrender. You can't hold on to your pain and expect God to heal you from it. Let go and let God, give Him your brokenness and He will put you back together right in front of the people that broke you. So let go and leave everything in God's hand because you will eventually see God's hand in everything.

– Noor Niami

Your Struggles Will Change Your Life

The struggles you are facing do not define you but they will shape the person you need to become in order to overcome them. In the middle of every difficulty lies an opportunity for growth. Your struggles will develop your strength and build your character, when you go through difficult battles and decide not to surrender then you have already won. You are not your struggles and you are not your mistakes so stop identifying yourself with them. It may be hard now but it will not always be this hard, it will get easier as you get stronger, and someday you will look back and realise your struggles have changed your life for the better and shaped the person you are today.

– Noor Niami

Be The Mate to Your Soul

Before anyone else can love and honour you, you must learn how to love and honour yourself first because your relationship with yourself sets the tone to every other relationship in your life. If you love and honour yourself then you will be capable and willing of letting people, who do not align with your truth and values, go. You set them free and you free yourself from partaking in their reality, which does not align with yours. You will understand that it is nothing personal if someone is unable to love you because you know that in order to love someone you need to love yourself first. So if they couldn't love you it just means they didn't love themselves. And you can't give that which you don't have, for out of the good treasure of your heart you bring forth what is good. So let go of your need for wanting to be loved by someone else and learn to love yourself. Become your own soulmate by mating with your soul, become the person you're looking for. Magic begins the moment you love and accept yourself.

— Noor Niami

Have Faith

Have faith that everything will work itself out because it will. You don't need to know the details of what, when, how, or where. You just need to relax and believe that things will fall into place and make perfect sense at the perfect time. Your job isn't to have it all figured out but to believe everything is unfolding according to a perfect plan for your life. Your faith will require you to see beyond what is happening, your faith will require you to call those things that are not as though they are. Speak victory over your battle. Speak peace over your chaos. Things can be crumbling down and you still have the ability to believe that something great is on the urge of happening. Things get worse before they get better but they always get better. Have faith in God, have faith in yourself, and have faith in life. All is well, relinquish control, surrender, and let go. Accept what is and have faith in what will be.

– Noor Niami

Singleness

People look down on singleness as though being single is a lack of options. Being single is in fact a choice. A choice you make that you're no longer joining the crowd and settling for less out of the fear of being alone. You would rather be happy alone than be miserable with someone else. Being single means you have options but you choose not to settle because your happiness and existence are not defined by a relationship status. You choose to live happy every day and let your happily ever after work itself out.

– Noor Niami

Don't Be a People Pleaser

Stop being anything other than yourself. Stop trying to please everyone because you will never be able to. It is not your job to please others just as it is not their job to please you. It is up to us to please ourselves and create our own happiness and joy and these things must come from within. It takes a lot of energy and effort to always be someone you're not but the minute you let go of who you think you need to be then you become yourself. Accept and embrace yourself with all your imperfections, flaws, beauty, and magic and let everyone see the real you. Once you accept yourself for who you truly are and stop being someone you're not then you will no longer seek anything from anyone and the need to please others disappears. You no longer need them to validate you because you are now validated from within and this is freedom at its best. So stop pleasing others and do more of what makes you happy. Always be yourself because you are beautiful and imperfectly perfect just the way you are.

– Noor Niami

It's Okay

It's okay to be confused, it's okay to be hurting, it's okay to be scared and finally it's okay to not be okay. Everything is okay, don't be hard on yourself. We all go through things we wish we didn't need to go through and face things we didn't want to face. But in the midst of all you're going through know and believe with all your heart that everything will be okay and you are going to be okay. It's okay if you don't feel okay. Don't force yourself to feel anything other than what you need to feel right now. Believe me when I say I know what it's like to lose everything in a matter of minutes and watch your life crumble in front of you as though it was a horror movie. There were numerous times where I wanted to just end my life and be done it with, I was in so much pain and turmoil I didn't know what to do other than watch my whole life break and shatter into a million pieces. I was devastated beyond anything I can ever describe and I didn't think I was going to make it but I did. As I look back now I still don't know how I got through what I went through but what I do know is that I never gave up on myself. So I want you to hang in there and don't ever give up on yourself because you deserve to be happy. It's okay if you don't understand it all, it's okay if you don't know where you're going, it's okay not having all the answers, it's okay to breakdown and have a meltdown, it's all okay. There is no right or wrong about any of this because you are doing your best in everything. You are where you need to be, you don't need to be anywhere else and you don't need to be racing with anyone else. Be okay with where you are and trust that everything will be okay in the end.

– Noor Niami

Note to Self

It's better not to have anybody than to have someone who makes you feel like nobody.

– Noor Niami

You Can't Heal Unless You Feel

Healing requires you to face the very things you have been running away from. Healing requires you to face your shadow, to embrace your darkness and to feel the pain no matter how painful it is. You cannot heal unless you feel because when you feel your emotions you are in essence acknowledging them, facing them and embracing them as your own. You have been running away from the painful parts of you but the more you run the more they will chase you. Running away from your pain will not make it go away but on the contrary your pain will grow bigger and deeper until it has caught your attention so you can address it, feel it, and heal it. Nothing ever goes away until we face it and it has taught us what we need to know. Your pain requires your company, your pain requires your attention and your pain requires your love. Running away from your pain is a race you'll never win, don't run but sit with it so you can feel it, heal it, and release it.

– Noor Niami

Be Grateful

Gratitude shifts your focus from lack to abundance, from what you don't have to what you do have. The more you are thankful for, the more you will receive. But the more you focus on what you don't have, then even what you have will be taken away from you and you will never have enough. Replace your complaining with thanksgiving and this will change your life. Gratitude will shift your attitude in appreciating everything around you and out of this state of being, only good things can come your way. If you have gratitude you will be given more, and you will have an abundance. If you do not have gratitude, even what you have will be taken away from you. So in all things at all times be grateful because gratitude is the best attitude anyone can have.

– Noor Niami

Fighting in Silence

Some battles you will fight in silence and some demons you will face alone. It gets lonely and hard but the battle you're in today is developing the strength you need for tomorrow. Where you are today is preparing you for where you're going tomorrow. And whenever you find yourself fearing and doubting how far you can go then take a moment to look back and see how far you have come. Everything you have faced, all the battles you've won, all the demons you've conquered, and all the fears you have overcome. Believe in yourself and all that you are because there is something inside you that is greater than any obstacle you face.

– Noor Niami

The Art of Letting Go

One of the hardest lessons in life to learn is letting go. You fight to hold on and you fight to let go. Letting go is a process and it is indeed an art because it requires certain skill sets to learn and master the art of letting go. We become prisoners of our own mind when we try to control the uncontrollable. We become prisoners of our past by wanting to change it and we become prisoners of our future by trying to control it. Here's one truth; what we try to control is in fact controlling us. The solution? Relinquish control, let go of the need to control everything, and trust that everything will work itself out. Control comes from fear, fear of loss, fear of rejection, you name it. But if you trust then you no longer need to control anything because your faith has now replaced your fear. And when you trust you let go and surrender and this is the key to being happy and at peace. It's important to understand that letting go is very well a process because you can't let go of something you've held on to for so long overnight. You let go bit by bit, you wake up every day and loosen up your grip a little, then a little more the next day. And little by little until you loosen your grip completely and release it. Therefore, letting go requires time and patience, love and kindness to yourself, and don't compare yourself to how quickly someone else has done it. You let go at your own pace and in your own way. The day you let go and surrender will be the day your life begins.

– Noor Niami

Be The Light

If there is one thing I want you to be certain of is this; there is light but not at the end of the tunnel, *you* will become the light in the tunnel. At some point you will need to stop looking for the light and decide to become it instead. Then you will become the light you have been desperately looking for and when you do, be sure not to let anything dim the light that shines from within. Your deepest darkness will lead to your greatest light.

– Noor Niami

You Are Evolving

As you go through adversities and hardship you will start to shift and change into a new person. You will begin to realise that you are not the same person you used to be. The things you used to tolerate have become intolerable. While you once remained quiet, you are now speaking your truth. Where you once battled and argued, you are now choosing to remain calm and peaceful. You are beginning to understand the value of your time and energy and there are some situations that no longer deserve your time, energy, and effort. You no longer cling to people who are no longer meant to stay in your life and you don't chase after anything because you know what's meant for you will never miss you and that which misses you was never meant for you.

– Noor Niami

Someone, Someday, Will Hurt You

It doesn't matter who you are or where you're from, someone, someday, will hurt you. That someone will take all that you are and rip it into pieces and they won't even stay to help you pick up the pieces. But through your breakdown you will have the opportunity to know yourself for the first time ever; you will see what you're made out of and how capable and strong you really are. Your breakdown will give you the opportunity to rebuild yourself, to become the person you were always meant to be. We all hit rock bottom but it doesn't mean we need to stay there. The only way to go is up from there and things will only get better for you from here on out. And those who hurt you and did you wrong have unknowingly made you strong and sometimes you have to get knocked down lower than you have ever been to stand back up taller than you ever were.

– Noor Niami

You Have Come a Long Way

Don't forget how far you've come. Don't be discouraged if you're not where you want to be but look at the fact that you are not where you used to be and thank God for that. See how far you have come and don't forget what it took for you to get here. Sometimes it was easier to just give up but you didn't and chose to push through instead. You've come too far to go back and you've come too far to settle so don't get discouraged, don't get frustrated and tired of waiting, your breakthrough is coming. You didn't come this far to only get this far and one day you will thank yourself for not giving up. Be proud of yourself for how far you've come and press on to the things that are ahead because the best is yet to be.

– Noor Niami

Nothing Ever Goes Away

Nothing ever goes away until you face it. Lessons in life will be repeated until they are learned. It is like being at school, you have to study, learn and pass the exam in order to move up to the next level. We are all being taught by the school of life and there are lessons we need to learn before we can graduate to the next level. Every level in your life will require a different version of you so with every new level you will need to shed an old layer of the person you are, to become the person you need to be. But most people don't allow themselves enough time to go through the process and they decide to run from one thing to another. But the situation will repeat itself, it might be different faces, different places but the experience will be the same. Don't make the same mistake, give yourself time to process what has happened and be patient enough to learn the lesson so you can graduate to the next level. Then you will realise there was a blessing in every lesson you learned.

– Noor Niami

You Will Find Love Again

You will find love again, but first, you need to find the love from within and be able to give it to yourself before someone else can come into your life and give it to you. Once you have mastered self-love then the love you will find will be everything you ever dreamed of and more. You will find a love that has the power to tear down the painful walls of your past so that both of you can build a new wall filled with beautiful and unconditional love. The love you once had was conditional but the one you will later find will be unconditional. You will find someone who makes your heart sing for joy, someone who you can trust as a result of you now trusting yourself. You will communicate and understand each other on levels that you never established with anyone before. The love you find will be genuine and selfless, the kind of love that will pour in you and never drain you. You will find the love you have been praying for and wishing for, the true love you deserve, the love that is free from any conditions. It is given and reciprocated freely and joyfully without expecting anything in return. A love so perfect in an imperfect world.

– Noor Niami

Be The Change

We've all made mistakes, we've all lied, we've all hurt others, we've all said things we later regretted, we've all fallen into temptation and faced the consequences of our poor actions. We've all been there, we've all been scared and our fear got the best of us. But we're also allowed to change, we're allowed to grow, we're allowed to fix our mistakes and become a better version our ourselves. We are not our mistakes. Our shortcomings do not define us because we have the ability to learn and change. We can all change and be better and do better. So don't let your past define who you can be today. Go ahead and change because you're allowed to make mistakes, learn from them, and grow. If we want to change our world, then we need to become the change we want to see.

– Noor Niami

Life is an Echo

What you send out, comes back

What you sow, you reap

What you see in others, exists in you

What you give, you get

Do not judge so you will not be judged

Give what you want to receive.

Life will always give you back what you are giving, it's a mirror of your own words and actions. Your life is not a coincidence but an echo of your own doings.

– Noor Niami

Release It to Receive It

You need to release what you want to receive. I know it sounds counter-intuitive but it is the absolute truth whether we choose to believe it or not. When we want something we hold on to it so tightly, we're constantly thinking about it, we're yearning for it and needing it but this is all counter-productive and it will actually delay it from coming to you. You cannot receive from a place of neediness because when you need something you are in essence saying I need this thing outside of me to complete me and make me whole. But this is a lie that must be replaced with the truth. The truth is that you are already whole and complete as you are and you don't need anything from the outside because you have everything you need on the inside. And until you truly believe and embody this truth then it cannot come to you. Life is trying to show you that everything you will ever need already exists within you so you must become what you want before what you want can come to you. This is what the word *become* is, you *be* it first and then it *comes*. If it's love that you're after then love yourself first. If you want a particular partner then be that partner to yourself. If you want success then see yourself as successful. And the biggest irony in all this is when you become what you needed you will no longer need that thing you thought you needed and that's when it usually comes.

– Noor Niami

Rise Up

To the joy in you, rise up

To the love in you, rise up

To the beauty in you, rise up

To the strength in you, rise up

To the light in you, rise up

To the power in you, rise up

To the wonder, magic and magnificence in you, rise up.

– Noor Niami

You Are Enough

Here is a reminder that you, just the way you are right here, right now is simply enough. You don't need to be anything other than what you are now to be enough. You are enough by simply being you. You are strong enough to make it through, you are brave enough and you are capable enough. Stop thinking otherwise and start believing in yourself. You are enough exactly as you are with all your flaws, weaknesses and problems. There's no need to change anything, all you need to change is the belief that you have to change. You are enough, you have always been, and you will always be enough. You just need to align your thoughts with the truth; that you are more than enough just the way you are.

– Noor Niami

Put Yourself First

At some point you need to decide to put yourself first and accept yourself even when others don't. You have to choose yourself above all else. Putting yourself first is not selfish but it is a form of self-love and self-care because you know you can't love and help others if you don't love and help yourself first. Don't set yourself on fire to keep others warm, let them light their own fire while you mend to yours. Don't be someone else's second option when you can be your own priority. Choose you because how you love and treat yourself is how you teach others to love and treat you.

– Noor Niami

Fear of Loneliness

It is better to be alone for a little while than to spend your life with someone who makes you feel alone. A lot of us have this huge fear of being alone and we accept just about anything at all cost. But why? What is this fear all about anyway? It isn't the fear of being alone that scares you, it is the fear of being with yourself. It means you are not at peace with yourself and you're running away from yourself rather than facing yourself. You don't want to be left alone with your demons. But what if I told you that's exactly where you need to be and what you need to be doing? Being alone with your demons so you can finally face them, conquer them, and stop them from running your life? Nothing can be changed until it is faced so if you want to overcome your fear of loneliness then you have to be willing to be alone for a little while. You overcome fear by doing the exact thing you fear. Loneliness is just an indication that you are in desperate need of yourself, that you are not at one with yourself and you are trying to find a home for your soul in someone else. But the home you seek is in you and you can choose to walk back home to you at any time because your inner being has been waiting for the moment you go looking for it. What you seek is seeking you.

– Noor Niami

Guard Your Heart

Guard your heart and be diligent with what you let consume your heart. Two opposing forces cannot abide in the same heart. Where there is fear, faith cannot abide. Where there is hatred, love cannot abide. Where there is selfishness, humility cannot be found and where there is unforgiveness, peace cannot be found. Light and darkness, good and evil cannot dwell in the same heart. So guard your heart diligently and choose wisely for everything you do flows from it.

– Noor Niami

It Takes Time

It took time to get to know someone and it took time to trust them and let them in. So it will also take time to forget them and let them go. And that's okay, take all the time you need because letting go and moving on from someone you invested so much of your time, energy and emotion into, won't be easy. You've held on to that person for so long so it will take time to let them go. It's okay to not be okay, and it's okay to hold on when you're not ready to let go just yet. There's no set time to do something that will take time so relax, breathe and take all the time you need. And remember just as we break in pieces we also have to heal in pieces too. Give it time.

– Noor Niami

Strength

Strength does not come from winning and having things go your way all the time. Your struggles and setbacks develop your strengths. When you go through hardships and decide not to surrender, this is strength. It's not in the rising up we get strong but in the fall. When we fall and decide to keep going, this is strength because strength isn't developed on your good days but rather your bad days. You don't need strength when you're flying high and doing well, you need strength when all the odds seem against you and you continue to press on and push through. This is strength. Strength is when you choose not to let the circumstances defeat you, that's when you will defeat them. No matter how much it hurts now, one day you will look back and realise your hardest times have led you to the greatest moments of your life.

– Noor Niami

Regret

Regret is a waste of time. Never try to hide who you are or what you've been through. Never be ashamed of what you had to endure, the only shame is to have shame. Always stand up for what you believe in. Never regret the past because the past has shaped you into the person you are today. There's a reason for everything. Every event, every person, every mistake, every bad thing that has happened to you, there is a reason for all of it. Grow from it, let it teach you and change you into a better person. We all make mistakes, we all struggle, we all have weaknesses but we are not what happened to us. We are more than our circumstances and we are more than the story we tell ourselves. Don't regret anything that has helped you in becoming who you are. The only thing you will regret is how much time you spent regretting things. And never regret being a good person to the wrong people. Your behaviour says everything about you and their behaviour says enough about them. Never regret anything; everything that happens is either a blessing, which is also a lesson, or a lesson, which is also a blessing.

– Noor Niami

You Were The One

Let me refresh your memory; you were the one who actually cared about them. You were the one who stuck by their side when no one else would. You were the one to stick around even when everyone told you to leave. You were the one who had their back through thick and thin. You were the one who loved them even when they gave you every reason not to. You would have done anything for them because you believed in them more than they believed in themselves. But you had to give up on them because they gave up on you first. Remember you were the one; you were the one to give them everything and got nothing back. You were the one for them but they weren't the one for you.

– Noor Niami

And Then It Happens

One day you wake up and you will be in this place. In a place where everything feels right. Your heart is calm, your mind is quiet, and your soul is at rest. Your thoughts are positive, your feelings are light, and your perspective is clear. You are at peace, at peace with where you've been, at peace with what you've been through and at peace with where you're headed. You are at peace with yourself, at peace with everyone else, and at peace with life.

– Noor Niami

Write The Story You Want

The past is the past; don't let it hold you back. Move forward and don't look back because what is ahead is bigger than what was left behind. You can't move forward by looking backward so every time we look back it will keep us from moving forward. Our past is a story we keep rehearsing and playing in our mind and once you realise that it is just a story then you have the power to change the story. The previous story may have been created without your input because at that time you weren't aware of the power you held to create your life. But now you're aware and you're awake so there's no reason why you can't begin again. And this time around you will hold the pen so you can write your story just the way you want it. But you can't start the next chapter of your life if you're busy re-reading your last one so at one point you will need to turn the page. When you finally turn the page you will then realise there is so much more to the book than the page you were stuck on.

– Noor Niami

Let Them Criticise You

Often people who criticise your life are the same people that don't know the price you paid to get to where you are today. Don't worry too much about them and what they say behind your back. Remember they're behind you for a reason because in the end you will never be criticised by someone who is doing more than you, you will only be criticised by those who are doing less. Don't let their jealousy and bitterness drag you down, their jealousy is their insecurity, not yours. Do more of what makes you happy and don't feel bad for making decisions that upset them. It's not your responsibility to make them happy, you are responsible for your happiness, not theirs.

– Noor Niami

Rescue Yourself

A lot of people go through life in pain, never really transcending their pain and ascending into a new trajectory of life. They don't allow themselves to heal because healing terrifies them. They have no idea who they are outside their trauma and pain because they didn't give themselves the opportunity to grow beyond the pain and find out who they really are. And it's okay to be scared but we must push through despite the fear because no one else is going to rescue us from ourselves, our demons, our insecurities, and fears. Only we can rescue ourselves by facing everything we fear because the only way to overcome fear is to face it. Love yourself enough to face your fears and set yourself free because no one else can do it for you. Only your self-love and courage can rescue you from yourself.

– Noor Niami

The Choice is Yours

You are being presented with two choices; evolve or repeat. When you evolve you grow and when you grow you overcome because the only way out of something is through it. The only way out of anything is going through it and coming out on the other side. But you cannot defeat what you don't want to face and nothing can be changed until it is faced. If you run, you repeat and if you face, you evolve and the choice is yours to make. What choice will you make?

– Noor Niami

Happiness is Letting Go

True happiness doesn't come from holding on but it comes from letting go. If you're mourning the loss of what you thought your life was going to be then let it go. Things will not always go as we plan and that's not necessarily a bad thing. You have to let go of the image of what you thought your life would look like and learn to enjoy the story you are actually living. You are exactly where you need to be right this moment so take a deep breath and relax. Trust that things have a way of working out in the end and everything is going to turn out better than you expected. That's what you call God's plan.

– Noor Niami

Lost

You may feel lost like you don't really belong in this world, you're right you don't. You are in this world but not of it, you come from above and you didn't come to fit in, you were born to stand out. Feeling confused and lost is part of your journey, you need to lose yourself to find yourself. You don't need to understand everything you just need to accept and believe that life is happening for you and it'll all make sense one day. You may feel lost and alone but know that you're not at all forgotten and there is a plan over your life. You needed to be lost to be found so breathe and believe that being lost is part of being found.

– Noor Niami

You Can't Change People

You can't change people who don't see an issue with their actions but you can refuse to let their actions change you. Don't let their bitterness take away your kindness and don't let their chaos steal your peace. Whatever you do don't be one of them but always rise above and be the better person that you know yourself to be. Always give love, respect, and kindness not because they deserve it but because that's who you are and don't be anything other than yourself. You can't change people who don't want to be changed so you either accept them for who they are or start living life without them. We may not be able to change people but we can change who we choose to be around.

– Noor Niami

Be a Leader

Be a leader of yourself and your life. Don't allow someone else to take the lead and lead you astray. You create your own reality so don't let someone else's limitation become yours and hinder your potential. Being a leader doesn't mean you see yourself better than anyone else or teach others how to live their lives. Being a leader is taking control of your own life, your own thoughts, feelings, and actions. It is about you being in charge of your own life. Take the lead and become the leader of your life before someone else does.

– Noor Niami

Count Your Blessings

Count your blessings no matter how big or small they are. Be grateful for what you have before what you have is taken away from you. Don't let your lack blind you from seeing how blessed you really are. Happiness begins when you start counting your blessings not your problems because a grateful heart is a happy heart and it's better to count your blessings than count your troubles and lose your blessings. Embrace your life, count your blessings and be grateful for what you have.

– Noor Niami

They Always Knew

Some say you don't know what you have until you lose it but I beg to differ. They always knew what they had but they never thought they would lose it. They believed that you will be there forever, forever holding on to them. They were not afraid to lose you because they knew no matter what you wouldn't walk away. They got too comfortable with depending on your forgiveness. Never let a person get comfortable with disrespecting you and crossing your boundaries, never lose yourself for anyone else. Let them go because when you let go two things can happen; they will either realise your worth or you will. Let them lose you because if they didn't appreciate your presence then let them appreciate your absence. They will regret the day they lost you and reality will hit them hard when they finally realise you were the best of what they had. They will try and look for you in everyone else but you won't be found.

– Noor Niami

You Are The Healer

No one else can heal you, only you hold the power to heal yourself. The healer you have been looking for is your own strength and courage in facing all your fears. Healing takes courage and strength because we are asked to face all our fears head-on. This isn't going to be pretty, this is going to be one hell of a messy fight but it will definitely be worth it. We all have wounds and some of our wounds have been there for years and decades even. So don't expect to heal what has been there for years in days, it is a process. Be patient and gentle with yourself because healing is messy but it will be the best thing you will ever do for yourself. Do it, heal yourself no matter how much it hurts. I assure you that it will get better, the darkness you're in today will lead you to your light. There is joy after your pain and there is life after your heartbreak. Keep going, take baby steps if you need to, crawl if you need to but whatever you do; do not give up on yourself. You deserve all the joy and happiness you have been looking for and all this is on the other side of your healing.

– Noor Niami

Wonderfully and Fearfully Made

You are a child of the living God

You are loved

You are known

You are seen

You are heard

You are worthy

You are valuable

You are beautiful

You are strong

You are smart

You are enough

You are one of a kind

You have a purpose

You are a masterpiece

Know who you are so you don't believe the lies of who you are not.

– Noor Niami

You'll Never Be Left Empty

God will never take anything away from you without the intention of replacing it with something much better. If He has asked you to put something down it is because He wants to give you something better. But you cannot receive what He wants to give you while you're still holding on to what He wants you to let go of. Obedience is an act of faith and every act of obedience brings with it a blessing. Sometimes God takes away something you never expected losing, but He will replace it with something you never imagined having. He will never leave you empty and will replace everything you lost. If He asks you to put something down it's because He wants you to pick up something greater. Let go and let God because what is coming is better than what has gone.

– Noor Niami

Acceptance

Acceptance is freedom, acceptance is peace, and acceptance is rest. When we no longer fight against anything, we surrender and accept it as it is. And when you accept a situation, you find freedom and peace. Accepting your past frees you from its chains, accepting your present frees you from its struggles, and accepting your future frees you from its worries. When you accept, you surrender, and when you surrender, you trust and when you trust, everything becomes possible for you. Accept where you are and where you are will change.

– Noor Niami

Revenge

The true mark of growth and maturity is when someone hurts you and you try to understand their situation and where that pain came from, instead of trying to hurt them back and seek revenge. We think if we avenge ourselves it'll make us feel better but I promise you it won't. Revenge comes with a high price, it brings with it guilt and condemnation and it will leave you feeling worse than you did at the start. You will discover that revenge is futile and the best antidote for revenge is forgiveness. Forgiveness isn't for them, it's for you. For you to release the anger, hatred, and bitterness from your heart and take back your power. Don't allow their actions to destroy your heart because no one has the power to destroy you unless you give it to them. Revenge keeps our pain alive but forgiveness heals us and liberates us.

– Noor Niami

Food For Thought

Behind every great man stands no woman because there is no greater man than the man who acknowledges the woman standing right next to him.

– Noor Niami

Focus on Your Journey

Silence the chatter inside your mind and quiet the voice that is constantly telling you who you need to be and where you need to go. Trust in your heart that who you are and where you are now is enough. You don't need to be someone you're not ready to be and you don't need to go somewhere you're not ready to go. Your soul knows best, it knows where you are in relation to where you want to be, it knows who you are to who you're going to be and all this will happen in its perfect timing. Forget about everyone else and don't compare yourself to them because you have no idea what their journey is all about. Happiness begins when you stop comparing yourself to everyone else and focus on your journey instead.

– Noor Niami

It's a New Day

Don't let your yesterday take up too much of today. Don't let a bad yesterday ruin your chances of having a good day today. Let it go because thinking about it and dwelling about what happened isn't going to change the fact it happened so don't contaminate your today with yesterday's disappointment. Let it go and start again, every day is a new day, a fresh start to begin all over again right from where you are. Every day is a new day, a new opportunity, a new chance, a fresh start so don't start your day with the broken pieces of yesterday. Every new day is the first day of the rest of your life, make it count.

– Noor Niami

They Will Tear You Apart

Some people will come into your life and tear it up, they will hurt you beyond anything you have ever experienced in your life, and you will feel pain like you've never felt before. You will no longer be the person you were before you met them, nor will you ever be the same person you were with them. The person you once were has died and the only choice you're left with now is to rebuild yourself up as a new person. This process of dying and being reborn hurts more than anything you could imagine because you will be having an identity crisis. Everything you thought to be true was in fact a lie and you will have to unlearn everything you've known in order to learn again. Only this time you'll be learning the truth and the truth will set you free. Don't be afraid to die on the inside in order to be reborn into your true authentic self. Yes you'll never be the same again but you will be so much better.

– Noor Niami

Live a Purposeful Life

Live your life with a purpose. Let all that you do be done with a purpose, with an intention, with a thought. Have a vision, have a dream because you need to know where you're going and what you're doing to get there. When you live life on purpose, when you do good and add value to everyone and everything around you, opportunities and blessings will present themselves to you and your life will become fulfilled. And instead of you being the one chasing, blessings will start to chase you and overtake you.

– Noor Niami

This is Your Life to Live

You can't let people scare you or control you. You can't go your whole life trying to please everyone. You can't go through life worried about what everyone else is going to think, say, or do. You can't let the judgment of others stop you from being you. Because if you do then you're no longer being yourself, but instead being someone everyone else wants you to be. Go ahead and live your life because it's time for you to live without worrying about the expectations of others. Go ahead live your life, take chances, and do more of what makes you happy. Don't let anyone make you feel guilty for living it, this is your life to live.

– Noor Niami

Don't Force Pieces That Don't Fit

Don't force anything because you become unhappy by forcing things. Some things are just not meant to be no matter how much you want them to be. Just let things happen and let life flow. Life has a weird way of working itself out you just need to take yourself out of the way, go with the flow and see where it takes you. Don't force things that are not meant to be. Let go, and allow what's meant to be to come to you effortlessly because the first step to getting what you deserve is by letting go of what you don't.

– Noor Niami

You Can't Love Someone Into Loving You

Here's the thing I learned the hard way; you cannot love someone into loving you. No matter how much you love them and how loyal you are to them it will not change them into loving you. They must be willing to change themselves and nothing you can ever do or say will push them into changing unless they truly want to. Because change requires growth and growth comes with pain and discomfort, and some people are not willing to go there, maybe not just yet. You can love them to the point of emptying yourself out completely and it won't be enough. Love is a choice you constantly need to make and you can't make it for them. Letting go of someone you love is going to be one of the hardest things you will ever do but I promise you holding on to someone who'll never love you back is even harder.

– Noor Niami

Hold On to Your Soul

Don't let a dark world steal away your light. Don't let the actions of others turn you into one of them. Don't let their coldness replace your warmth and don't let their pride and ego turn you away from your loving and gentle spirit. Certain things are bound to happen, things that will leave us hurt and confused. People will be unkind and unfair; they will hurt you and abandon you but don't let any of these things make you unkind. It's okay to be sad and grieve, to start questioning life and wonder why did all this happen to you. But what's not okay is for you to join the world against you and become one of them. What's not okay is when you let others turn you into someone you're not. No matter how hard things get, hold on to your soul and heart and never let them grow cold or weary. Knowing that what doesn't break you will, in fact, make you, and this too shall pass. Hold on to your values and continue to be a person you are proud of.

– Noor Niami

You Are Bigger

You are bigger than your pain,

You are bigger than your challenges

You are bigger than your mountains

You are bigger than your mistakes

You are bigger than your past

You are bigger than your fear

You are bigger than your heartbreak

You are bigger than anything that is set to come against you. It's time you stopped playing small and walked into the fullness and greatness of who you were created to be.

– Noor Niami

Worrying

Worrying is a waste of time. It doesn't change anything, it makes things worse. It messes with your mind and steals your peace because you are trying to control the uncontrollable and this is a battle you'll never win. Let go of what you cannot control and trust that everything will work itself out. Worry does not empty tomorrow of its sorrows but it empties today of its strength, it steals your chances of being happy today. If we want to be happy and have peace then we need to stop worrying because you can't worry and be happy at the same time. Don't dwell in the past and don't worry about the future, focus on living in the present moment because this is all you have so make the most out of it. Don't wait for things to get easier, simpler, or better but learn to be happy with what you have and trust that what you want will come to you. Worry ends when faith begins.

– Noor Niami

Blaming is Powerless

It's so much easier to blame someone else for all our problems. It's better to give them the responsibility than to take responsibility ourselves. Especially if we are not willing to face and own up to whatever the problem is. But running away is never the answer. You start to blame others when you are avoiding some truth about yourself that you are not willing to accept as your own. So we blame others and make it their problem when in reality it is ours. Don't blame anyone or anything for your situation or problems because this will take away your power to change it. When you blame others you are saying you are powerless over your own life which is not true. You hold the power over your life, no one else does and the first empowering step to reclaiming your life is by taking responsibility. The moment you accept responsibility for your life and the moment you stop being a victim to your circumstances is the moment you regain the power to change your life.

– Noor Niami

A Choice

Someday someone will come into your life whom you will love more than life itself. You will be willing to lose it all for their sake but won't fathom the idea of losing them. You will fight against the world for them and you will hold on to them for dear life. Nothing and no one can stop you from loving them and you will ignore every red flag shown to you because in your eyes they are perfect and they can do no wrong. You will put them on a pedestal above anyone else, even above yourself. You will begin to worship them as though they are your god, the source to your well-being and existence. You will believe to the deepest core of your being that you are meant to be together forever and that they're your happily ever after. But one day; things will go horribly wrong and the life you planned with them will crumble and shatter into pieces in matters of minutes. The person you thought you were going to spend the rest of your life with has turned out to be the very person you now need to run away from to save your soul. You have given them all of your heart and they didn't just break it, they crushed it. When that day comes it will be a choice between you and them; holding on to them and losing yourself, or letting them go to save yourself. And when that day comes I really hope you choose yourself.

– Noor Niami

Not Every Loss is a Loss

Believe me when I tell you that not every loss is a loss. Don't be scared to lose some people and some things. We cannot gain something without giving something in return so be okay with losing some things to gain things of much greater value than what you've lost.

You will lose someone and find yourself

You will lose your ego and find your soul

You will lose hatred and find love

You will lose expectation and find forgiveness

You will lose worry and find peace

You will lose fear and find faith

You will lose your mind and find your heart

You see not everyone and everything you lose is a loss but at the loss of something you will in fact gain something greater. Your biggest losses will turn into your biggest gains.

– Noor Niami

Look and See

Before crumbling to the ground; stop. Stop and look at how far you have come and all it has taken you to get here. Stop and see that you are not in that horrible place you once used to be in. Stop and see the strength you needed to cultivate to keep moving forward even when you were on the verge of giving up. And you didn't give up; you're still here standing and moving forward. Recognise the strength you have inside of you, the strength and wisdom you have gained along the way. You can do this, not because you aren't scared but because you will continue on strongly despite your fear.

– Noor Niami

Your Growth Frightens Them

You're allowed to change, you're allowed to be a different person today than the one you were yesterday or the one you will be tomorrow. Don't feel bad for evolving and growing just because others are not willing to grow. With growth comes a bit of pain and discomfort and some have chosen to stay in their comfort zone instead. Let them do what's best for them and you do what's best for you. If people are still holding on to the old you then this is their problem and not yours to worry about. Don't carry their burden and make it yours. They want to see you do well but they don't want to see you do better than them because your strength will remind them of their weakness. Accept this as part of life; some people will be for you and some against you. Either way don't feel guilty for outgrowing them and even outshining them. They too can be the same or do the same if they choose to but it's something they need to do, you can't do it for them. Don't let their insecurities slow you down, keep going. Your growth frightens people who have no plans on changing.

– Noor Niami

Out of Love or Loneliness?

Are you choosing to be with someone out of love or loneliness? Because the two are very different yet we seem to confuse them as the same. You won't know the answer to the question until you have learned to be alone with yourself. When you are comfortable with being on your own and enjoying your own company, then you will know if you are choosing someone out of love or loneliness. It might hurt to walk away from someone but it will hurt more if you stay somewhere you don't belong. Don't let your fear of being alone keep you in a lonely relationship. The pain of being with someone who makes you feel alone is more painful than being on your own. Don't be afraid of losing someone who isn't afraid of losing you. There are times when alone is the best place to be.

– Noor Niami

God's Plan

As much as you want to plan your life, it has a way of surprising you with unexpected things that will make you happier than you originally planned. This is what you call God's Plan. Sometimes the bad things that happen in our lives put us directly on the path to the best things that will ever happen to us. Let go of your plans and let life strengthen you. No matter how much it hurts please know and believe in your heart that the pain won't last forever and nothing leaves your life unless something better is coming to replace it. Have faith in God's plan because He has plans to prosper you and not to harm you, plans to give you hope and a future.

– Noor Niami

Lessons And Blessings

Your overwhelming breakdowns will lead you to your biggest breakthroughs. Your hardest lessons will bring you your greatest blessings. Your hardest times will lead you to the greatest moments of your life. It may not look like it and it certainly won't feel like it at the start because they will be blessings in disguise at the beginning. Often times life takes us in a direction we never saw ourselves going but it will turn out to be the best road we have ever taken. You may not understand what is happening right now but later you will. Sometimes what appears to be a problem is actually an answered prayer in disguise also and when things are falling apart they may actually be falling into place.

– Noor Niami

Stop Caring About What Others Think

The minute you stop caring about what others think will be the minute you start being yourself, freely and joyfully. The greatest prison people live in is the fear of what other people think. But at some point you need to stop caring about what people think and care more about what you think because what we think of ourselves determines who we become. Don't waste your time worrying about them, listen to what you want, do what makes you happy because this is your life to live not theirs. People will always have an opinion and if they judge you it's because that's how they treat themselves so don't take it personal. The way they see you is the way they see themselves. Follow your heart, listen to that inner voice, and stop caring about the opinion of others. Because the day you stop caring what other people think of you is the day you begin to be yourself and live your life.

– Noor Niami

Let's Be Honest

The problem wasn't them, it was us. We made excuses for their bad behaviour, we accepted their obvious lies, and we gave them another chance, again and again. We sold ourselves short, we didn't believe we deserved better, and we stayed too long. We made the mistake of letting people stay in our lives far longer than they deserved and yes we learned the hard way; but we learned.

– Noor Niami

Today I Choose

Today I choose to forgive myself. I choose to accept myself. To be myself. To love myself. To appreciate myself. To respect myself. I will no longer force things that are not meant to be, I will no longer knock on closed doors. I will no longer beg people to stay in my life. I choose to let go of people whose company affect my peace and I choose to let go of those who weigh me down. I choose to forgive those who hurt me. I choose to forgive myself also. I choose to forgive myself for holding on to people for longer than I needed to. I choose to forgive myself for hurting myself by holding on to the pain longer than I needed to. I forgive myself for not knowing what I know now, and today I choose to set myself free. I choose to liberate my soul and rise above the ashes that were meant to bury me. I choose to be happy. I choose to be me. I choose to be beautiful.

– Noor Niami

Fear of The Unknown

The biggest human terror is that of the unknown. We are creatures of habit and we'd rather stay with who we know and what we're familiar with even when the people and situations turn toxic. We allow toxic people to remain in our lives and tolerate toxic situations because we would rather cling to the known then let it go and surrender to the unknown. But true growth and development come from letting go of the known and embracing the unknown. In the process of letting go of what is known you will lose many things from the past but you will find yourself. Don't be in a rush to have it all figured out, learn to trust the journey even when you don't understand it and let life surprise you. You won't know what you're capable of if you don't embrace the unknown and find out what you're really made out of.

– Noor Niami

Your Surroundings

You become what you surround yourself with; choose carefully because you will become your environment. Your surroundings can help you grow or make you shrink because you are a product of your surroundings. Is your surrounding making you bitter or better? Is your surrounding helping you grow or making you shrink? Is your surrounding leading you in the right direction and most importantly is your surrounding bringing you peace or chaos? You can't change the people around you but you can change who you choose to be around. Surround yourself with what you want to become and be around those who bring out the best in you.

– Noor Niami

An Apology

Don't let anyone's ignorance, hate, drama, or negativity stop you from being the best person you can be. You need to accept that some people will never admit they were in the wrong. They will never recognise their mistakes and learn their lessons. Some people will never really grow so you will never see their behaviour change. Sometimes you just need to let them be and move on without any closure because there comes a time to stop trying to make things right with the wrong people and accept an apology you never received.

– Noor Niami

Love Yourself

Make a decision to love yourself right here right now. Love is not a feeling; love is a choice we make. Choose to love yourself so you don't have to spend your life looking for someone to fill cracks that shouldn't be there in the first place. We can't expect someone else to fill our cup when we're not willing to fill it up ourselves. It's not about finding someone to give us what we need it's about us giving ourselves what we need. It all starts and ends with us, no other person can grant you what only you can grant yourself. The love you seek is already within you, it's there but you can't see it because your traumas and wounds are covering it. Peel off the layers that are not you, be willing to dig deep because deep within you lies a great treasure. But you need to dig deep first so you can find it. It's there, it's always been there, and it's who you are. You have come from love, you are pure love, but first peel off the person you are not so you can organically become the person you truly are. The love you seek can only be found in you and it's not about finding someone to love you, it's about you learning how to love yourself.

– Noor Niami

You Reap What You Sow

Yes they hurt you and disappointed you on so many levels, yes they didn't turn out who you thought they were but don't hurt yourself the way they've hurt you by holding on to the pain. Forgive them and set yourself free, never give in to hate and let it turn you into someone you're not. Let it go, set it free, and karma will take care of the rest. There is a beautiful principle about life; you reap what you sow which means we get what we deserve and must eventually face the consequences of our actions. So they will certainly face the consequences of their actions towards you but that's not for you to worry about. Your job is to pick yourself up, heal from the pain they caused you and move on to living a happy life. Let karma do its thing while you go on about living your best life.

– Noor Niami

Believe in What You Want

We all desire and want things that have not yet manifested into our physical world. We all have dreams that are yet to come to pass and we're all waiting for one thing or another. Life will cause you to ask for things and reach for more because you are constantly evolving and growing and as a result our desires and wishes change with us. Whenever you ask for something you must believe in what you're asking for. When you ask it is given in the spirit realm because God has finished all the work from the beginning of time. Everything you will ever need or ask for already exists or else you wouldn't be able to conceive the desire in your mind. So if you come to terms that everything you are asking for already exists and it is already done then you won't doubt your desire but believe in its realness. You don't need to work for it because it's already done; you just need to receive it by faith. Everything that is given onto us is given by grace and unmerited favour so all you need to do is receive it. It is yours but you need to believe it before you can receive it. Otherwise, you cannot receive something you don't believe in, that's impossible. Anything you ask for, believe you have received it and it will be yours. Your faith is the key to your answered prayer.

– Noor Niami

You Cared Too Much

You see here's the thing; you shouldn't have to fight for someone who isn't willing to fight for you. It's as simple as that but we complicate it. We try and justify why they are not fighting for us and give them excuses when we should just see it for what it is and not make it something it's not. Don't fight and lose yourself in the process when they're not willing to lift a finger for you. They love being fought for but they wouldn't do the same for you. This should tell you that you cared too much and they didn't and there was the problem. Know when to fight and know when to give up the battle and walk away. If they don't fight for what they want, let them cry for what they've lost.

– Noor Niami

Who is Holding You Back?

The only one holding you back is yourself. There is no one else stopping you other than yourself. You may think it's because of what someone else is or isn't doing but the truth is it's because of what you're doing. The only reason why we may believe someone or something else is holding us back is because we have given our power away by believing they are holding us back. It's the power of that belief. No one is holding you back but you are using them as an excuse to hold yourself back. You are the only one who holds the power to either move forward or hold yourself back. If you believe that you can or can't, you are right in both cases because whatsoever a man thinketh, so is he. We hold ourselves back because we are so afraid of failing. But failure is not in doing something and failing at it, it is in doing nothing that we fail ourselves.

– Noor Niami

In Love With a Lie

We can waste our whole life waiting for them to change. Being with them yet feeling alone and wondering why they won't treat us right. We keep blaming ourselves and giving more and more, hoping that our efforts will change things. But the truth is; we're in love with a lie, a dream, an illusion, a never-will-be. This is the truth and the reality we are denying but sooner or later we need to face the fact that no matter what we do it will never be enough. We can't love people into loving us and we can't fabricate the truth with a lie. Once we accept the truth, we will begin to let go and it will be the best decision we make.

– Noor Niami

Always Choose

There will be times in your life when you have to choose between being loved and loving yourself. Always choose loving yourself because no one else can love you more than you love yourself.

– Noor Niami

You Are Being Prepared

Everything you are going through is preparing you for something great. Everything you are going through is preparing you not just for what you asked for but so much more than anything you've asked for or even imagined. Every story, every person, every event to the smallest detail, was meant to happen and nothing happened by accident or mistake. There is no such thing as a coincidence or luck, there is a plan over your life and everything is working together to bring this plan to pass. Everything you have been through has helped you become the person you are today. For every new level in your life will require a new empowered version of yourself. Everything you are going through is preparing you for something so great beyond what your mind can conceive or your heart can believe. Trust the process and have faith in the journey. Be patient and kind to yourself in the process and learn to enjoy the journey and not be so fixated on the destination. It's not about the destination; it's always about the journey.

– Noor Niami

Infidelity

Infidelity brings with it an excruciating pain to the person who is being cheated on. It is one of the worst, if not the worst, betrayal of trust and boundaries. Being cheated on is brutal and the pain hits you deeper than people realise. It destroys you temporarily, it destroys your outlook on life and what you thought was once real has turned into a big lie. You begin to question your sanity and worth. The event may have happened once but the images of your beloved and the person he or she has committed the act of infidelity with will haunt you, making you live the experience over and over again. Infidelity makes you feel that you are not good enough, that this somehow may have been your fault. Your self-esteem drops to the ground feeling unworthy of being loved. All these feelings are normal and it's okay to feel like that for a while because the one you loved the most has hurt you the most. But don't stay in that miserable place for too long and sooner or later you will need to stand back up and realise that what they have done had nothing to do with you in any way. A person's actions are a reflection of one's character and there is absolutely nothing wrong with you but everything wrong with them. You are beautiful, you are worthy, and you deserve someone to love and respect you. So be sure to love and respect yourself enough to know that you deserve better.

– Noor Niami

Don't Beg For Human Decency

You shouldn't have to beg someone for things that should be given freely. If you catch yourself begging for human decency; time, respect, compassion, kindness, and some understanding then you need to step back and realise you shouldn't be begging anyone for anything and certainly not for the bare minimum. Don't beg for love, don't beg someone to be with you and don't beg for attention, commitment, time, and effort. Don't beg them to stay or come back. You should never have to ask for these things because these are given freely to the one you love. Nothing you can do or say will force anyone into doing something they don't want to. Begging is demanding and degrading, it diminishes your worth and character. Life has taught me that no one, absolutely no one, under any circumstances, is ever worth begging for and losing yourself for. Let them go and hold on to yourself with love, dignity, and respect.

– Noor Niami

You Hold The Power

You hold the power to start over and create the life you dream of. No matter what anyone else has done to you, where you came from, or what has happened to you, you hold immense power, now more than ever, to start all over again and create a life beyond your wildest imagination. We all have our stories and we all have been through things we wished we didn't need to go through but the truth of the matter is every single one of us has a story and a past but we are not our stories, neither are we a product of our past. We are far beyond any story and any event that occurred in our lives. You hold the power to stop overthinking about people and situations that instantly bring you down. You hold the power to walk away from drama, manipulation, and conflict. You hold the power to go through anything and come out of it on the other side, and you hold the power to stop giving it away to people and things outside of you. You hold the power to create an abundance of everything you want; love, joy, happiness, blessings, and all sorts of miracles. To get there you need to let go of the old story and create a new one. You need to realise the power you hold to radically transform your life. The power is yours to create the story you want, all you need to do is stop creating the story you don't want.

– Noor Niami

Let Them Go

Stop letting people who do so little for you control so much of you. Have you ever been in a situation where someone who does so little for you controls so much of your mind, will, and emotions? I have, and it's not a pleasant place to be in because not only are they doing so little for you, they also expect so much of you in return. They feel overly entitled and they expect you to just keep giving because their entitlement is rooted in their delusion of superiority, self-centeredness and selfishness. You will continue giving out of your kindness and generosity but it will never be enough because you can't be grateful for something you feel entitled to. So my advice to you is to let them go because they are toxic to you. Let them go because they take and take and leave you empty. Let them go because they are the anchor that's drowning you whilst you're trying to stay afloat. Stop giving the same people different opportunities to disappoint you.

– Noor Niami

The Choice is Yours

Every test in our life makes us bitter or better.

Every problem comes to break us or make us.

Every pain presents itself to hurt us or heal us.

Become a victim or a victor of your circumstances.

You make the choice.

– Noor Niami

Confidence

Self-confidence is the most important and attractive quality a person can have. How can anyone see how beautiful and special you are if you can't see it yourself? And when I say beautiful I am not talking about outer appearance because true beauty is seen in one's soul and heart. Having self-confidence doesn't come from the way you look, or the way you dress, from what you have, or what car you drive. Self-confidence comes from knowing who you truly are as a person and accepting yourself completely. It comes from loving yourself unconditionally, flaws and all and trusting in your abilities and qualities. Self-confidence comes from you feeling so secure within yourself, self-assured and self-validated. If you don't know who you are then you will believe every lie about who you are not. But when you know yourself, when you love yourself, and when you value and respect yourself, you are now the most beautiful and confident person in this world.

– Noor Niami

True Love is The Answer

True love is the answer to everything. It is the answer to all your pain, it is the answer to all your problems, and it is the answer to all your fears. It is the answer to everything and the only reason for anything. If you are experiencing anything other than love then you need to stop doing what you've always done; judge and criticise yourself, and start loving and accepting yourself. We don't allow ourselves to feel the love that already exists within us because we have believed in a lie that says 'I need to find someone so I can love and be loved.' But the truth is; you don't need anyone, you just need to begin to love yourself because no one can love you into loving yourself. This is your greatest responsibility; to love yourself and to know that you are enough just the way you are because in order to love and be loved by someone else you must first love yourself.

– Noor Niami

Reserving a Space

Stop making excuses for their lack of character and poor actions. They can't appreciate something of value so why bother asking them to value your worth? Don't let who you believe someone is deep down excuse the reality of how they are making you feel right now. Choosing to see the best in people is a sign of your kind and loving heart but don't let your heart blind you from seeing the truth. Sometimes your heart needs more time to accept what your mind already knows and that's okay, give it time. But sooner or later you will need to stop making excuses for their lack of character and poor actions because a person's actions will tell you everything you need to know about them. When people treat you like they don't care then please believe them because if someone wants to be a part of your life, they'll make an effort to be in it. Otherwise don't bother reserving a space in your heart for someone who doesn't make an effort to stay.

– Noor Niami

Forgive Your Parents

The way we grow up and the people we become has a lot to do with our parents and our upbringing. As children we need a certain level of tender, love and care. But when parents fail to meet a child's needs then he or she grows up believing there must be something wrong with them. Most of our traumas stem from childhood because we have been taught to live life from the outside in and no one ever taught us that life can only be lived from the inside out. We might blame our parents for who we have become but here's the thing you need to know and accept as the truth; your parents were doing the best they could with the understanding and awareness they had. They were dealing with their own demons at that time. They couldn't teach you something they didn't know and they certainly couldn't give you something they didn't have. If they didn't love themselves there was no way they could have taught you how to love yourself. You didn't have a choice as a kid but now you do. You can be bitter and resent them or get better and forgive them. It gets easier to forgive them when you know they gave you the best of what they had at the time even if what they had was little. Forgive them for being as flawed as everyone else, they were trying their best. Now you do your best to heal and stop the cycle of trauma and pain from passing down to your kids.

– Noor Niami

Arrogance

The arrogant, judgmental, and egotistical appear to think they are better than you. Truth is; they are attempting to convince themselves that they are. They are prideful, self-deceived, and full of themselves. Their pride goes before their destruction and their haughty spirit before their fall. They are a curse upon themselves and they must live with themselves for the rest of their lives. Don't let their arrogance ruin your kindness because arrogance is for the weak and kindness is for the strong. When they treat you poorly, don't take it personal because it says nothing about you but a lot about them. Don't be fooled by who they appear to be. Those who appear the strongest are actually the weakest and those who appear to be most confident are actually the most insecure.

– Noor Niami

Make This Moment Perfect

Stop waiting for the perfect moment and make this moment perfect. We wait for the right time, or for the right person before we allow ourselves to be happy but why should our happiness be based on an outward condition. Let your happiness be unconditional because true happiness comes from the ability to be happy no matter what is happening outside of you. We can only control what's going on within ourselves and if we let go of what we can't control then we can be free to enjoy this present moment without any condition. I speak for myself; I used to live a very conditional life, I used to say I can't be happy until I get this or that (whatever it is for you). I always made an excuse of why I can't be happy now and sure enough I wasn't. It wasn't until I stopped waiting to be happy and just decided to be happy. I didn't care about where I was or where I was going, I no longer worried about who is in my life or isn't. I let go of all expectations, conditions, and rules and decided that I am going to be happy unconditionally because I deserved to be happy. Happiness is a choice, it's a decision you make; that you're not going to wait for the perfect time but make this time perfect to be happy. Let go of all your conditions, your reasons, and your excuses to why you can't be happy and just be happy. Don't wait for life to be perfect, otherwise you'll be waiting your whole life.

– Noor Niami

Selfless Love

Love others without expecting them to be different, help others without any reason, and give without expecting to receive something in return. No one was ever miserable by loving and helping others. Don't be ashamed of having a kind and generous heart, live by your values and truth despite what anyone else is doing for you. You love because that's what you do; you are kind because that's who you are. Don't let someone else's inability to love take away your ability to love. Stay true to who you are, live by your values and uphold your morals because being a good person was never a bad thing.

– Noor Niami

Be Proud of Yourself

Not in a boastful or prideful way but in a loving way; be proud of the person you have become because you have had to go through hell becoming him or her. Be proud of the person you are today compared to the person you were yesterday. Never let the mistakes of your past define you but let them shape you into a better version of yourself. You will realise what's important and what isn't, you will worry less about what people think of you and care more about what you think of yourself. You will look back and you will realise how far you've come, how there were times you didn't think you were going to make it through, but here you are standing on your two feet again. Smile and be proud of yourself and the person you have fought to become because indeed you went through hell becoming who you are today.

– Noor Niami

Your Peace is More Valuable

Learn to choose your battles wisely and be protective of your peace. You don't need to show up to every battle you're invited to. Some battles are not worth fighting for and losing your peace over. Your peace is far more valuable than being right; and right in whose eyes? Does it matter? If you keep your peace then you have just done what's right in your eyes and that's all that matters. Not every situation requires your attention and energy. Don't let something that isn't important cause you to lose something important. Don't argue with ignorant people, they will drag you down to their level where chaos and disorder exists. Remain in your high level where peace and serenity exist. After all this is why they want to fight with you, to make you lose something they don't have so you can join them in their world of misery. Be smarter and wiser than them because anything that costs you your peace is too expensive and the less you respond to negative people the more peaceful your life will become.

– Noor Niami

Some Days

Some days are just bad days, that's all. You have to experience sadness to know happiness, you have to experience bad days to appreciate good days, and you have to go low to rise high. It's okay to not feel your best every day and it's okay to have bad days. Don't regret a day in your life and learn to embrace every day because good days bring you happiness and bad days give you experience. Both bring with them something valuable to you. And remember; it's just a bad day, not a bad life, and tomorrow is a new day.

– Noor Niami

What's Meant For You Will Be Yours

Doing nothing often takes you to the very best of something. When you do nothing, you stop worrying, you stop overthinking, you stop questioning, you stop analysing and planning. You stop being a stumbling block to yourself and take yourself out of your own way. Often times we stand in our own way blocking the very thing we want from coming to us. We believe we need to do something in order to get something but sometimes all you need to do is be still and do nothing so what you want can find its way to you. We believe we need to work for it but some things you just need to receive by grace. Therefore some things will require you to do nothing other than receive the blessing that has been predestined for you. What's meant for you will never miss you and what's meant for you will always be yours.

– Noor Niami

You Gave it Your Best

You have every right to be disappointed and heartbroken when things fall apart. It's okay to be sad, it's okay to be disappointed and hurt. It's okay if you miss them and it's okay if you wish things worked out differently. It's okay not to be okay and your feelings are real and valid. Allow yourself to feel without any judgment and bless all your feelings without fighting them. But never ever blame yourself for not trying hard enough, because truth be told; you did. You gave it your absolute best, you kept giving until you had nothing else to give. You gave it your all, you gave it your best and even that wasn't enough. So now let them go because it'll be the best decision you make. One day someone else will come and appreciate you and treat you the way you should be treated.

– Noor Niami

It Doesn't Get Easier

It doesn't get easier; you will get stronger. Life doesn't get easier, it may feel like it is but that's only because you are getting stronger. What used to make you stumble and fall no longer does and your falls have in fact made you strong. Your struggles have developed your strength because when you go through hardship and decide not to give up, this is strength at its best. When we cannot change our circumstances then we need to change how we react to them and often God will use our circumstances to change us. Our hardships change how we think and react to circumstances and the circumstances we want to change will actually change us. And although things don't get easier you become better equipped to deal with them because our suffering will produce endurance, and endurance produces resilience, and resilience produces character. And our character can only be developed through the experience of trial and suffering. Remember diamonds are made under pressure.

– Noor Niami

God is Within You

God is not this thing or a person you find somewhere out there. God can only be found in you. God exists in all of us, He is in us and all that there is. The reason why we can't find Him is because we are so busy with everything else and the noise outside stops us from connecting within. God cannot be found in noise and restlessness. God is found in silence, peace, and calmness of one's mind and heart. Have a look at nature for example; everything grows and exists in silence and we need silence to be able to connect with God. If you are looking for God then turn your gaze inward because He lives in you. He is only one thought away and one feeling away. If you seek Him, He will be found by you because He is always with you whether you're aware of it or not.

– Noor Niami

You Are The Creator

You have the power to create your reality. Your power to think, feel, and choose your reality regardless of what others are or aren't doing. Everything you perceive in the physical world has its origin in the invisible, inner world of your thoughts and beliefs. To become the creator of your reality, you must learn to control your mind; it all begins with your thoughts. By doing so, you will be able to attract into your life that which you intend to have and experience as you come to know the truth that your thoughts create your reality. Your life is the perfect mirror of your thoughts, beliefs, and dominant actions. Change what you believe in, and you will change what you do, and what you do will change your life.

– Noor Niami

The Beauty of Pain

Love Does Not Hurt

Everyone says love hurts; I used to believe this too. But this is
not true because true love does not hurt; true love heals. It's not
love that hurts; it is the rejection that hurts, the envy that hurts,
the loneliness that hurts. The truth is; love is the only thing that
covers up all pain and perfect love casts out fear. Love is the only
thing that does not hurt so if you are hurting then rest assured it
isn't love. Love heals, love makes you better not bitter, love makes
you more of who you are and less of who you are not. If it isn't
doing this for you then it isn't love.

– Noor Niami

Greatest Victory

Where your biggest battle is, there will also be your greatest victory and blessing. No one is perfect and everyone struggles. If you come across people who tell you they have a perfect life then they're lying to you. They are nothing but foolish, conceited, and self-deceived people. We all struggle and have battles, we all suffered from one thing or another and we all have had a mountain to climb and a battle to fight. But here's the thing; where your biggest battle is, there will also be your greatest victory. There is a blessing in the pressing because to get to the next level of your life your spirit has to be stretched. Don't be discouraged by the pain because your pain is an indication that something new is being birthed through you. The stretch is the preparation ground for what's coming and you needed to be stretched not only to obtain the blessing but also to be able to maintain it. Promotion is a process and you'll find that most of your transformation will happen during the preparation period. Hang in there and trust the process because you are being prepared for what you asked for.

– Noor Niami

The Beauty of Pain

You Were Born to Stand Out

We've all been rejected by people and especially those whom we wanted to be accepted by the most. The people we try to please and seek approval from are actually the ones who reject us the most. I couldn't understand why I was being rejected at the time but now I do. I didn't belong there and had they accepted me I would have settled in a place I don't belong in with people that are not my own. Here's the truth; some people will reject you purposely so you don't fit in and the only choice you're left with is to stand out instead. You weren't meant to fit in and be like the rest, you were born to stand out and be different so don't ruin that by being like everyone else. You are chosen, and set apart so don't try to fit in places that don't fit you and don't beg people to stay that are not meant to stay. Had God not ruined my plans for fitting in with the wrong people, my plans would have ruined me. So I thank God a million times for ruining my plans before my plans ruined me. And here's the thing I want you to remember; some people are going to reject you simply because you shine too bright for them and here's what you do; keep shining anyway!

– Noor Niami

It Can't Rain Forever

Let me assure you that you didn't come this far to only get this far. You didn't endure the storm so you see no sunshine. God didn't bring you all this way to only just leave you mid-way. If He brought you to it He will see you through it. Keep going and don't stop until you get there. Don't give up on yourself because what's coming will be far better than what's gone. The rain will stop, the winds will settle, and the sun will rise again. Hang in there and be strong because things will get better, it might be stormy now but it can't rain forever.

– Noor Niami

Clothe Yourself With Humility

We all struggle with pride. It's okay to be proud of ourselves to some extent but what's not okay is when we start to see ourselves better than someone else simply because we have something they don't have. Pride is poison to your soul because the gratification you get from your own achievements is temporary and it will always leave you empty wanting more and seeking more and nothing will ever be enough. It is the lack of gratitude and appreciation that will have you spiral down. Pride stops us from reaching our potential and moving forward with God's plan. It hinders our growth and delays our destiny. We need to let go of our pride and clothe ourselves with humility. To be humble is to be meek and to be meek is to be gentle and kind. When you are humble you are also thankful for all that you have and when you appreciate life then life will just get better for you. Humility is not a trait of weakness; humility and meekness are strength and they carry spiritual powers. When you are humble you are beautiful because nothing is more beautiful than the unfading beauty of a gentle and quiet spirit.

– Noor Niami

Be The Better Person

They get offended when you treat them the same way they treat you. They hate when you show them how it feels to be treated the way they treat you. But here's the thing I want you to know; how they treat you doesn't define you, it defines them. How they treat you is how they treat themselves because their actions are a direct reflection of their character. Don't treat them the way they treat you because you don't want to be like them. Don't give them a taste of their own medicine but give them a taste of your own medicine. Be the better person because you are of a noble character, don't degrade your character just because they're degrading theirs.

– Noor Niami

The Battle is Within

The hardest battle is the one between your ego and your spirit, so the battle is within you; between you and yourself. You are not fighting with people or circumstances, it may feel like it but I promise you the battle is actually happening within you. And you can't fix something from the inside when your gaze is set outside. You need to turn inwards to be aware of what is happening inside of you. To be at peace mentally, physically, and emotionally, we often need to be at peace spiritually first and this can only be attained by going from within. Your real life is the one you have inside of you and your outer life is nothing but a reflection of the one within. If you want to change your world, first focus on changing your inner world. Then your outer world will begin to shift to reflect your changes. Our external world is only a mirror for our inner world; what we believe in and how we treat ourselves. To change the outside world, you have to go deep inside and uproot the old beliefs that are no longer serving you. This isn't going to be easy but if you want something you've never had then you need to do something you've never done. And slowly but surely you will overcome your biggest enemy; yourself. And when you overcome yourself you have, in fact, overcome the world.

– Noor Niami

A Mistake

Loving you wasn't a mistake, but thinking that you loved me was. And I'm not sorry for loving you but I'm sorry for you not wanting that love. And when you start to miss me, I want you to remember one thing; I didn't walk away, you let me go.

– Noor Niami

Take Your Dependency off People

You had to be broken so you can take your dependency off people and put it in God. It hurts when you are broken down to literally nothing but that false shell had to break in order for the new you to emerge. Your ego had to die so your spirit can take over. Sometimes God has to break us down completely in order for us to be put back together as a new person. And the reason why we're broken and hurt in the first place is because the people we loved and trusted the most have hurt us and betrayed us the most. And why wouldn't they? They're only humans and we shouldn't have depended on them to give us what only God can give us. We depended on them for our happiness and wellbeing; they became the source to our life and then we wonder why things went horribly wrong. No one can take the place of God and we can't look for ourselves in other people. You must take your dependency off people and put it in God or else you will always be dissapointed. Learn to love the Creator more than the creation and when you take care of your relationship with God; God will take care of everything else.

– Noor Niami

It Will Be Worth It

No one said it is going to be easy; but it will be worth it. For nothing worth having comes easy because great things take time. Here's the thing I want you to know; you will reach your destination but how you get there is something you can't control. We all start off with our own plan on how we wish to get there but life will never cease to surprise us and it will take us down a different path than the one we have set out. Life does this to challenge us, to strengthen our faith, and build our character. It bends us and stretches us so we become flexible and not rigid, set in our own ways. It teaches us how to adjust our sail to the wind. So life may not always take you through the easiest way but I assure you it will be the best way for you. And once you get to your destination you will have an epiphany that it was never about the destination but always about the journey and the person you have become. Trust the journey even if you don't understand it because it will all be worth it in the end.

– Noor Niami

Be Your Own Hero

Be your own hero; don't play the role of a victim, but become the hero of your story. Hold yourself back, or heal yourself back together. The choice is yours. Don't wait for someone else to acknowledge you, to notice your talents, or believe in your potential because you could be waiting a long time. Become the hero you're looking for, be the person you need to be, and believe in yourself even when no one else does. Don't assign someone else to be the hero of your life because you are the hero of your own story.

– Noor Niami

Don't Give Up

You're allowed to scream, you're allowed to break down and cry, but you're not allowed to give up. Don't give up on yourself, you have been through so much, don't just throw it away and give up. It's hard yes, some days will be harder than others yes, but don't ever give up or give in. You may not have had the start you would've hoped for, but this doesn't mean your finish won't be better than anything you could've hoped for. It's not about how you start it's about how you finish, and difficult roads always lead to beautiful destinations.

– Noor Niami

Scattered Pieces

Some days will leave you shattered on the floor with all your pieces scattered into a million pieces. You will begin to question your own truth and whether in fact what you've believed in is the truth. You will question everything you've once believed, you will look at the shape of your own soul and this is a good sign. It means you are ready to change, you no longer want to live life the way you have been living it. Whatever you do, do not run away from pain. Just sit with it and let it rip you apart, let it rip the person you are not, so you can become the person you were meant to be. It will be okay I promise you, you will be okay given that you don't give up halfway and go back to what broke you. Don't get lost in your pain, know that one day your pain will become your cure and often it's the deepest pain which empowers you to grow into your highest self.

– Noor Niami

Thank You

I thank you for the person you have helped me become. I thank you for not loving me because you helped me learn how to love myself. You didn't love me; you just loved the idea of having someone loving you. You didn't fight for me because you loved being fought for instead. You didn't value me but you taught me how to value myself. Thank you for not being there when I needed you the most because you taught me that I am in need of myself. I thank you for being who you were because you helped me become who I am. You led me back to myself, you led me back to my soul and you led me back to my God. And for that, I thank you.

– Noor Niami

You Have a Big Heart

No matter what life throws at you don't let it harden your heart, but on the contrary; let it soften your heart and make it gentle and kind. Don't let the world dim your light and don't let the hardness of others destroy your kindness. You have a big heart, full of love and compassion. Don't let another person's inability to love change your ability to love and forgive. Don't hold grudges, forgive often, and love more. Don't let anything steal your peace, let go of what you can't change and set yourself free. You can change the world; don't let the world change you. Let go of everything but hold on to your good heart because it is your biggest treasure.

– Noor Niami

Sandpaper

Sandpaper is used for smoothing and polishing and some people will come into your life to do just that. They will come into your life to show you another layer of yourself that needs to be shed. When people walk into your life, they are either going to be a blessing or a lesson but even in the lesson there is a hidden blessing. They will bring your unconscious into the conscious so you can finally see it and deal with it. They will bring your darkness to light so you can face what you can now see. Don't despise those difficult people in your life; they will actually cause you to grow the most. Just like the sandpaper is used for smoothing and polishing something, those difficult people will smooth and polish all your rough edges and you'll be shining and polished in the end. You were a diamond in the making and they were the pressure used to make you into one. Now do what a diamond does, shine!

– Noor Niami

Note to Self

Sometimes a man's purpose in a woman's life is to help her become a better woman, for another man. And sometimes a woman's purpose in a man's life is to help him become a better man, for another woman.

– Noor Niami

Forgive Yourself

Forgive yourself for not knowing what you didn't know before you lived through it. Living through what you didn't know has helped you know what you know now. So don't regret anything that has happened in your life because every person, every event, every situation has helped you become the person you are today. Don't hide from the shadows of your past and don't be trapped in the shame of your mistakes. Whatever you've done before, accept it, and let it go. Accept the fact that you are not perfect and you are capable of making mistakes. Forgive yourself because you were doing the best of what you can back then, and it's only when you forgive yourself you can begin again.

– Noor Niami

Worth The Pain

The best thing you can ever do for yourself is heal! Healing is one of the most important journeys you will ever embark here on earth. As a matter of fact you are here to do just that; transcend your limiting beliefs and ascend into a higher level of consciousness. We have all developed certain patterns of behaviour due to a belief programming we inherited from those around us when we were little. When we grow up these old false beliefs and patterns of behaviour are no longer working for us, they are now causing more harm than good. And as adults it is now our responsibility to heal ourselves back to wholeness. And healing of that kind will have you go deeper than ever before, uprooting everything that shouldn't be there right from its roots. It will get messy and it will be painful but the joy, the freedom, and the beauty you later gain will be so worth the pain. The best thing you can ever do to yourself and to everyone around you is to heal yourself and become whole and complete from within. Love yourself enough to heal yourself even when it hurts, your love will heal your pain.

– Noor Niami

Your Only Competition

The only person you should be competing with is yourself because you are your only competition. It's always between you and yourself. You might think it's between you and someone else but it never is. The battle, the struggle, is in your mind. You could be your worst enemy or best friend and you get to make that choice. It's not about what everyone else is doing, because what they're doing is irrelevant to your journey and progress. If you compete with others, you will become jealous and bitter. But if you compete with yourself you become better. Become a better person than the one you were yesterday and dedicate yourself to becoming your best version.

– Noor Niami

Not All Storms Come to Disrupt

When you are around people who are toxic in nature and abide in strife, conflict, and disharmony then God is nowhere to be found amongst them. And where there is no God, there is no grace and where there is no grace there is no strength, love, joy, and peace. In a nutshell, God is not there! We become who we surround ourselves with and if they are low in nature then we will go down with them. God wants to promote you and elevate you into a higher dimension but He can't do that when you're constantly being dragged down into a lower dimension. What you want can only be found high up. What you need is above; where love, joy, and peace abide and you can't rise up when you have people constantly dragging you down. Being around toxic people is detrimental to your soul and wellbeing; it hinders God's plans for your life and delays your destiny. It's usually around that time when a disaster usually happens so it rids you of some people that you couldn't get rid of on your own. So not all storms come to disrupt our lives; some come to clear our path.

– Noor Niami

Trees And Seasons

The leaves may fall, but the tree still stands because it has strong roots. Remember trees lose their leaves every year and they still stand strong and wait for better days. So, if you feel like you're losing everything, remain strong and stand tall because better days are coming. The best thing about life is that everything you've ever lost will be replaced with something better so don't let the pain of one season destroy the joy of all the rest.

– Noor Niami

Narcissistic Abuse

Narcissistic abuse is a spiritual healing lesson of the highest order. It's when your life is being torn apart and broken down by the narcissist to literally nothing so you can rebuild a new life once you have healed and emerged into a new person. The narcissist comes into your life to hit the very parts of you that are hurting you. They rip apart your wounds and leave them wide open, giving you an opportunity to heal once and for all. It is about reprogramming us from everything we thought to be real. It is about the transformation and renewal of our mind, thoughts, and emotions. Stepping onto a more evolved path; a path to becoming our True Self. Here's the truth; the life with the narcissist was never meant to work, it was always meant to wake you up and heal you. The narcissist was only there to show you the unhealed parts of you so you can own up to them and heal yourself from your traumas. You might not have gotten to that level of healing if the narcissist hadn't been presented in your life. They become the necessary stepping stone in becoming your true empowered self. It grants you the incredible opportunity to create the new you; the real you and a new life that is now aligned with the real you. You become empowered, understanding that no-one, but you, is responsible for your fulfillment, safety, and wellbeing. And you will never again assign anyone else that much power over your life. This is the other side of narcissistic abuse; this is the highest form of spiritual healing, this is freedom and liberation at its best.

– Noor Niami

Stop Waiting And Start Living

Stop waiting for someone to fall in love with, stop waiting for that perfect job, stop waiting for the weekend, stop waiting for tomorrow, stop waiting for life and start living life. When you stop waiting for anything this is when you will begin living. Don't waste your life waiting, start living because life is happening right here, right now but you're missing the now by waiting for tomorrow. Don't miss the present moment by dwelling in the past or worrying about the future. Today is a gift, appreciate it, live it, and make the most of it because the future depends on what you do in the present.

– Noor Niami

This is Your Pain

No one can tell you how to feel or process your pain because this is your pain to feel not theirs. They don't know how deep your pain is, they don't know how long your pain has been there, and they certainly don't know how much this pain is hurting you. They are not the ones to feel your pain, they are not the ones to fight your battles, and they are not the ones breaking down. You are, this is your pain not theirs. Don't feel ashamed that you're in pain; be proud that you're facing the pain when everyone else is running away from theirs. Be proud of your pain, for you are stronger than those who have none.

– Noor Niami

Self-Partnering

Self-partnering is the foundation for all other relationships because it all starts with the relationship you have with yourself. Being self-partnered is an essential key to achieving a healthy relationship with self, life, and others. It is important to be safe and healthy in your own body, to live a life free from old abusive patterns and be able to generate what you need from within. When you become self-partnered you take full ownership and responsibility for yourself and wellbeing, for your joy and fulfillment. When you partner up with yourself you are then able to heal yourself from the wounds of not feeling lovable, heard, respected, and treated with care. You will become the person you needed when you were young. Your True Self is waiting to be uncovered by you once you have lifted out of the heavy traumas that have been stopping you from becoming who you really are. Once you discover your True Self you will realise how incredible and powerful you really are, how loving, kind, and generous you are. And you've always been that, you just had to uncover your darkness to get to your light.

– Noor Niami

You Are Worthy of Love

Others' inability to love you doesn't mean you are not lovable. But for them to love you they need to love themselves first. And if they don't love themselves then they certainly can't love you. You cannot give of something you don't have. Our relationship with ourselves is the foundation of all other relationships in our lives so they couldn't give you something they couldn't give themselves. Don't let their inability to love you make you question your self-worth to be loved. You were and always will be worthy of the love you give to others, so don't regret having a good heart but let them regret losing a good-hearted person like you.

– Noor Niami

Believe in Yourself

When you feel like stopping think about all the reasons why you started in the first place. When you feel like giving up and calling it quits, think about how far you've come. Only we can push ourselves because no one else is going to do it for us. Your dreams are yours to believe in and your journey is for you to go through. Don't compare yourself to others because their journey is different to yours. Keep going and don't give up until you get what you want, and get to where you want to be. Great things don't come from comfort zones and you need to lose the good to make room for the great. Believe in your dreams, believe in yourself, and don't give up until you get there.

– Noor Niami

Listen to Me

As broken as you may feel, you are still strong. With everything you lost, you have gained something else. Without the darkness you couldn't discover your light, and without your pain you wouldn't know joy. You may be bent but you are not broken because nothing has the power or permission to break you. You might be scared but you are not hopeless because eventually your faith will get bigger than your fear. You may be weary but not powerless because you are far more powerful than you think you are. Your battles will lead you to your victories and your struggles will show you your strength. Everything is working together for your highest good and greatest joy. Even when life doesn't seem to be working out for you, it is.

– Noor Niami

Hold On to Your Truth

When you know someone is a liar then why believe in what they're saying when everything they say is a lie? Why believe in what a liar says when there is no truth to be found in them? Why make someone else's lies become your truth and why equate your self-worth and value with someone like that? Don't let someone's lies make you doubt your own truth and never argue with someone who believes their own lies. Hold on to your truth, hold on to your honesty, and hold on to your integrity because these are valuable things a liar can never have.

– Noor Niami

I Know How It Feels

Believe me; I know how it feels when everything in you is hurting. I know how it feels when all you want to do is lock yourself in your room and drown yourself in your tears. I know how it feels when you want to scream from the top of your lunges. I know how it feels to cry in the shower and scream in the pillow so no one can hear you. I know how it feels when you wait for everyone to go to sleep so you can fall apart and wish you were dead instead. I know how it feels when everything is hurting you, your heart is broken, your soul is torn and your spirit is crushed. I know exactly how it feels. Do whatever you need to do, process the pain your way because there's no right or wrong way. How you feel is how you feel, so breathe and do what you need to do for now because we all process pain differently. But I promise you; from the bottom of my heart, from someone who's been where you are, things will get better! It won't always be like this and your best days are ahead of you. Everything is going to turn out better than you expected given that you keep believing and keep going. This too shall pass.

– Noor Niami

I Am Not the Same

I am not the same person you used to know. A lot has changed, I have changed. I am not who I was with you because you broke me time and time again. You took the old me and broke her down; you put her to death, so you left me with no choice but to raise myself up anew. I am not the same person, with the same soul or the same heart you once used to abuse. The pain you hurt me with has made me stronger; I have grown, and I'm not the same person you once knew. You don't even know me anymore and you'll never get the privilege of getting to know who I am now.

– Noor Niami

Silence The Judge in You

You have spent all your life judging yourself but why not start approving of yourself instead? What's the worst that can happen? There's nothing worse than judging and punishing ourselves. We all have a judge inside of us who is the first to judge and condemn us for everything we're not doing right. But you need to stop agreeing with this voice and start accepting and approving of yourself instead. Only then can you silence the judge in your mind because your voice of approval will be louder than the voice of judgment. Don't join forces by condemning and judging yourself. Be okay with making mistakes because you will and this is absolutely okay. No one is perfect so accept yourself as you are because the only thing holding you back is the idea that you need to be someone else. Let your voice of approval be louder than your voice of judgement. When you approve of yourself you will stop seeking approval from others and that's when you find happiness.

– Noor Niami

They're Not Who You Thought They Were

Have you ever thought so highly of someone that you put them on a pedestal? I mean they were your answered prayer and you were so sure that they were 'the one' for you. Nothing and no one was going to convince you otherwise because you've never been surer about anything else. If you've been there then you know the disappointment and heartbreak you endure when you realise they're not who you thought they were. They're not the person you made them out to be. How do you come to terms and accept the fact that you have invested all your heart, soul, time, and effort into someone who is not real? Of course you will be devastated and you will start to question how could you not see through the cracks? But the truth is; there were many red flags but we chose to ignore them because we didn't want to believe in something we weren't ready to accept. But eventually you need to let go of the illusion of who you thought they were and see them for who they really are. You can spend weeks, months, and years overthinking a situation trying to glue the pieces back together and justifying what could've, should've been. Or you can let the pieces go and move on to creating a new story, more beautiful than the one you were on before.

– Noor Niami

Never Stop Believing

Hate no one no matter how much they've hurt you. Live humbly no matter how wealthy you become. Be hopeful no matter how hopeless life may seem. Give much even if you've been given little. Treat others how you want others to treat you. Forgive all and forgive yourself and never stop believing that you are destined for great things. Pause, breathe, cry if you must but keep going because the best is yet to be and what is coming is going to be so much better than what's gone. Never stop believing that great things are going to happen for you.

– Noor Niami

Who Says You Can't?

Don't let someone else's limitation become your own. Who can tell you what you can or can't do? Only you can decide whether you can or cannot. Sometimes people will try to devalue and belittle you so you don't recognise your power and your greatness. They see it and are well aware of it; they just don't want you seeing it. Sooner or later you will recognise the power you hold and no one can stop you then. Don't worry about what other people think of you because there will always be some people who want to see you fail because they can't succeed. But I'm here to remind you; yes you can. There is nothing you cannot do unless you tell yourself you can't. So forget their jealousy, throw away the negativity, work on yourself, and don't look back on those who are trying to hold you back. They are behind you for a reason. They told me I couldn't; that's why I did it.

– Noor Niami

A Beautiful Being

Don't regret loving even if you loved the wrong one. Don't regret being a good person to a bad person. Don't sit there wishing you didn't love them or what a waste of time it was. Because time is never a waste when you love, time is only wasted when you don't love. Love is who you are and what you're made out of so don't regret being yourself even to those who least deserved it. Always love and be kind because your ability to love means you have that love inside of you. It's what makes you who you are, a beautiful human being.

– Noor Niami

Time Doesn't Heal

Everyone says that time heals all wounds but I disagree because it's not the time that heals your wounds; you learn how to heal them in time. It isn't the time who heals it's what you choose to do in time that will determine whether or not you heal. This is why most people go on about life the same way they always have because they weren't able to heal their wounds and transcend their pain. They've chosen to adapt and repeat instead. They too had the time but it's what they chose to do with the time that determined their course of life. We are given the same time, it's up to us what we choose to do with it. Heal and grow or repeat and remain the same. Time doesn't heal all wounds; you heal your wounds in time.

– Noor Niami

Raise Your Standards

What you tolerate becomes your standards and your standards create your life. If you always accept 'less than' what you want, then life will always give you less than that which you want. You will begin to think that you are unworthy of life's best and something must be wrong with you but that's not true. It's only because you are accepting less than what you want rather than refusing to accept less and wait for the best. You see, what you accept becomes your reality. So if you tolerate someone else's poor behaviour and participate in a toxic pattern then you are making this your reality by tolerating it and participating in it. You need to refuse participating in what you don't want and be able to confidently say 'this is *not* my truth', let it go, and move on. And when you begin to accept nothing but the best; the best is what you will start to get.

– Noor Niami

You're Learning

You're slowly learning that reacting doesn't change anything. It won't make things better, it won't make people respect you and treat you any differently. It won't change people, it won't change what happened but you can change what's happening now by the way you respond. You're slowly learning it's better to just let things be, let people go, don't ask for explanations, don't seek answers, don't fight for closure. You're slowly learning that life is better when you don't center it on what's happening around you but what's happening inside you. You're slowly learning that your inner peace is far more valuable than driving yourself crazy trying to understand why something happened the way it did.

– Noor Niami

You Were Everything

You were everything they wanted and everything they lost. You were the love they'll never feel again. You were the greatest beauty they'll never see again. You were the blessing they'll never get again, and you were the lover they'll never love again. You took on their pain as yours, you thought more of them than you, you broke yourself trying to fix them, and you lost yourself by holding on to them. They didn't deserve you and you deserved better. They'll attempt to replace you with another, they'll try and compare you with everyone they meet but they'll soon find out there's no one like you. They lost the moon while counting the stars and you were everything they wanted but couldn't keep.

– Noor Niami

You Are Whole

You don't need someone to complete you because on a deeper level you are already whole and complete. It's your belief of being incomplete that's standing in your way. You believe you need someone else to complete you, you believe you are incomplete; you believe you need something out there to make you feel whole. This is a false premise because the truth is; you have everything you need right now. You are a complete, whole, and total person lacking in nothing. Your wholeness must be known and lived by you, you must believe that you are already complete and you need to align your thoughts with this truth. No one else can complete us and it's not their responsiblity to make us feel whole, it is ours. If you want to be complete then start by changing the way you see yourself. Don't wait for someone to come and complete you because you are already whole and complete within yourself.

– Noor Niami

Don't Settle

Have you ever been told that you are too picky? Chances are you get told this by the people who have chosen to settle rather than wait for they actually want. Have a look around you and see how many people have chosen to settle rather than wait? You will find that a lot of people have chosen to settle for an okay life because okay is comfortable. But I'm here to tell you that you have every right of being picky because this is your life, your time, and your energy. Set your standards high and don't settle for less than what you want. It's better to wait for what we want than settle for what's available. Be confident in who you are and what you have to offer, and you're allowed to choose carefully who you offer this too. It takes a strong person to wait and not settle in a world that is accustomed to settling with anything just to say they have something. Don't settle.

– Noor Niami

The Narrow Gate

There is glory beyond the narrow gate but few are those who find it and even fewer are those who are willing to travel it. Not everyone will find their way and very few are those who find it and decide to walk through it because the gate is narrow and hard is the way that leads to life. And because the gate is narrow you won't be able to fit in with all your baggage so you will need to let go of many things and travel solo. You can't take with you things like anger, strife, unforgiveness, bitterness, hatred; all these cannot come with you. The narrow gate will cost you your old life, it will cost you people and things, it will cost you your old self, and it will change your life from everyone else. The journey may be hard but the harder the journey the better the destination and the harder the battle the sweeter the victory. The question is; will you choose to travel through it?

– Noor Niami

Stroke of Luck

Remember that not getting what you want is often times a wonderful stroke of luck because not getting what you want will turn out to be the best thing for you. And one day you will look back at everyone you've known and everything you've been through and bless every person, every situation, and every detail that was a part of your journey. You will forgive those who hurt you because if they hadn't tried to break you down you wouldn't have known you were unbreakable.

– Noor Niami

Let Life Surprise You

Life happens and we are given two choices; go against it or go with it. We can choose to go against it, struggle, and never get anywhere or we can choose to flow with it and let it take us somewhere. Resistance and struggle come from you trying to control the situation when all you're asked to do is surrender and let life do its thing. There will be things that we don't want to happen but have to accept, things we don't want to know but have to learn, and people we can't live without but have to let go. Life may not always go the way you'd planned or hoped for but that's no reason to give up on yourself just because things aren't happening for you right now. Things may not always go as planned but you still need to make the best out of what you have. We need to let go of the life we have planned so we can receive the one that is waiting for us. And if something isn't happening now it doesn't mean it will never happen. Everything will come to you at the perfect time. Surrender and let life surprise you in the most delightful way possible.

– Noor Niami

Hurting People Hurt People

Sometimes the reason why we need to let them go is because they can't help but hurt you during this phase of their life. When you love someone deeply you're able to also see them deeply and learn what demons live within them. And you realise the reason why they are hurting you is because they are hurting somewhere within themselves. A battle is raging within them and they may not even know it. So they take it out on you and fight with you rather than fighting the demons within because the battle is inside of them. This is when things turn toxic and you need to let them go. Not because you didn't care or love them but because the both of you can find the healing you truly need without being together and hurting each other in the process. Letting go doesn't mean you gave up; letting go means you set yourself and them free.

– Noor Niami

What We Want is Not What We Need

Sometimes God will give you exactly what you wanted just to show you it's not at all what you needed. And sometimes we need to experience what we thought we wanted only to realise it's not what we actually need. Then we return to God humbled knowing we don't always know what's best for us and that's when we normally surrender, let go, and let God. God's ways are higher than our ways and His thoughts than our thoughts. We need to let go of what we think we want so God can give us what we actually need. And at some point you just have to let go of what you thought should happen and let what's meant to be, be.

– Noor Niami

You Are a Caterpillar

Just when the caterpillar thought the world was over, it became a butterfly. All butterflies must go through a complete metamorphosis and in order to grow into an adult they go through four stages and each stage has a different goal and purpose to achieve. And the same thing goes for you; all your seasons have a purpose and they are all fundamental to your growth. And when you are in a season of isolation and loneliness, then that's when you are being prepared to fly. So never lose faith when life gets turned upside down, it will all work out in the end. Just when the caterpillar thought life was over that's when life actually began.

– Noor Niami

You Can't Be Strong All The Time

Don't expect to be positive all the time and don't force yourself to feel anything other than what you need to feel. Being positive and happy all the time is unrealistic. Trying to be positive all the time means you have to prevent negative feelings altogether and this isn't right because you must embrace all your feelings not just some. You can't expect to prevent negative feelings altogether and you can't expect to be positive all the time. You can't be strong all the time, sometimes you just need to allow yourself to be weak and let your tears out. Life will give you good days and bad days, and with every day you will still need to show up and embrace it. Lift the burden off yourself and don't try to be positive all the time because even 'trying' has a negative connotation on it. Let go, and be who you need to be in that moment because strength includes knowing you can't be strong all the time.

– Noor Niami

Focus on Yourself

Take your focus off other people and focus on yourself. That's how you set yourself apart, that's how you progress and succeed in life. No one ever succeeded by looking at what the other person was doing; your success is determined by what you choose to do. Worrying about where other people are in life and comparing yourself to them isn't going to change a single thing in your life. So, worry less about what they are doing and focus more on what you're doing, your dreams, and your vision. Kick your own goals in your own time because the only person to compete with is the person you were yesterday. Focus on you and do your thing.

– Noor Niami

Your Beliefs Create Your Life

If you want to change your life then you must begin by changing your beliefs because your beliefs create your life. It's not just merely thoughts; it's the thoughts you *believe* in. We get so many thoughts in a day and if we don't believe in them then they have no power in our lives, only our agreement grants them power. If we don't believe these thoughts then they are merely thoughts. But if we agree and believe these thoughts then they become true to us and you create from what you believe in. You cannot change yourself without changing your belief system first. Start with your beliefs; and your beliefs will change your emotions, and emotions will change your actions, and your actions will produce the result. You become the creator of your own life when you start choosing what you want to believe in. You can't change what's happening around you until you start changing what's happening inside you.

– Noor Niami

The Beauty of Pain

You Will Miss Me

And someday you will understand how valuable I was but by then it will all be too late. I might have been worthless to you but you'll miss me when I become priceless to another. I may have lost someone who didn't love me, but you lost someone who truly loved you. You will look for me inside of everyone you're with but you will not find me. You will search for me in every person but I won't be found.

– Noor Niami

Hope

Let your hope shape your future, not your pain. When you hope you choose to see light in spite of being surrounded by darkness and once you choose hope everything becomes possible. No matter how dark it becomes, how painful the journey may get, hold on to hope because it will be the very thing you need to get you through what you're going through. When things seem to fall apart, they're actually falling into place and sometimes you have to go through the lowest lows to get to the highest highs. Always hope, always believe, and always love. Never lose hope because your hope will never dissapoint you.

– Noor Niami

Take Care of Yourself

We are so busy trying to take care of everyone else we forget the most important person to take care of; ourselves. You deserve to be taken care of as well, you deserve to have all your needs met. And where we go wrong is we put ourselves and our needs on hold until we can find someone to take care of us. But no one can take care of you like you can. No one knows you better than you do; no one knows what you need more than you do. You know your soul, you know your heart, and you know what you need. Don't wait until you find someone, don't wait until the timing is perfect, and don't wait for tomorrow but start taking care of yourself now. You deserve the tender, love, and care you give to others. Take care of yourself because no one else knows what your soul needs more than you.

– Noor Niami

I'm Proud of You

I don't think people realise how much strength and courage it takes to pull yourself out of a dark place. To rebuild yourself up after you've been broken. If you did this today, or any other day, I'm proud of you. I'm proud of you holding yourself together when everything in you is falling apart. I'm proud of you still standing on your two feet after everything you've been through. I'm proud of you for not giving up when giving up was easier. I'm proud of the person you are fighting to become. And if no one else is; I am proud of you and you should be too.

– Noor Niami

You Deserve Better

You deserve a relationship with someone who never has you guessing where you stand with them. You deserve someone who is going to treat you like you matter every day not just when it's convenient for them. Don't waste your time trying to make things right with the wrong one but instead move on with your head held up high because you deserve better and you can do better. When you're with the wrong person everything seems like it's hard work, and everything is a struggle. Nothing seems to work the way you want it to and that's because you're in the wrong place with the wrong one. When being with the right person you don't have to work so hard at it, it shouldn't feel like it's hard work, things will just happen and move effortlessly. Things fall in place and make sense without you trying to guess everything or make anything happen. The moment you start to wonder if you deserve better, walk away because you do. Don't let people stay in your life far longer than they deserve. Don't let their indecisiveness about you make you wait longer than you need to. Their indecision is a decision, remember that.

– Noor Niami

Mind Over Matter

Age seems to be a big factor in everyone's life and they let their age dictate where they go and how far they go in life. People say things like 'I'm too old for this' or 'it's too late for me' and I am guilty as charged with this. I used to think the same; I used to think that my life is over now that I'm in my 30's. Crazy right? Here's the thing though, your age and how old you are is just a mind over matter thing. If you don't mind then it doesn't matter. Your age doesn't stop you from being successful; it's your mindset that is stopping you. Your mindset of letting your age control what you do and how far you go. But if you can just overcome this mindset and change your perspective then you can still be, do, or have whatever you want. It's never too late because we are all given the same hours in the day and you can start from where you are. Your age does not dictate your life; it's your mindset so don't mind it and it won't matter.

– Noor Niami

Social Media

Social media is an illusion, it's not the real deal and it certainly isn't real life. Don't get me wrong social media has given a lot of people the platform to do what they love but the negative side of it has made people compare their behind-the-scenes to someone else's highlight reel. They are comparing their real lives with those on social media and the sad thing is they are envious of things that don't even exist. The relationships, the lifestyles, most of these don't even exist. Life is far from perfect and don't let someone else's perfect picture make you believe they have a perfect life. As a matter of fact, some of the most famous people you see on social media are in fact the loneliest but you wouldn't know that because that's not what you see online. Don't compare your real life to that of an illusion. Your life could be so much better than theirs and you wouldn't even know it. Be thankful for what you have because you could be having something they desperately need but don't have.

– Noor Niami

Not Everything That Shines is Gold

Don't trust everything you see because not everything is what it seems. Not all that you see with your eyes is all there is. There are things beyond what your natural eyes can see and just because you can't see them it doesn't mean they're not real. Remember not everything that shines is gold and salt may look like sugar but they're very different. You meet people who promise you the world but in the end, they are the same ones who break your world. You meet people who promise to love you and never hurt you, yet they are the ones who break your heart and hurt you like no one else has ever done before. Don't be fooled by someone's outer appearance or who they say they are. Their actions will show you who they truly are. Actions speak louder than words and there's a message in the way a person treats you; just listen.

– Noor Niami

The Beauty of Your Heart

When you have a good heart you love too much, you trust too much, you give too much, you help too much but here's the thing you need to know; not everyone will have your heart. Those who have a good heart seem to hurt the most because it's not easy having a good heart in a cold world. The people you love will hurt you but you can't let those people change you. Don't let them change your heart and never regret having a good heart because no beauty shines brighter than that of a good heart. Be who you are and you will get what you deserve.

– Noor Niami

Little Tiny Steps

Take all the time you need to heal emotionally; moving on doesn't happen overnight and letting go doesn't take a day. It takes a lot of little tiny steps in the right direction to be able to break free from your broken self and your shattered dreams. We all process pain and heal differently so there's no set guideline on how to heal. It's a journey, and it's a process and you need to take it day by day. Do the best you can then let go of the rest and believe that one day you'll get there. It's okay to fall but be sure not to stay there for longer than needed. Eventually, you're going to have to dust yourself off, get yourself back up and put one foot in front of the other. Maybe you couldn't stop yourself from falling down but you can help yourself by getting up. Falling down may not have been your choice but staying down is.

– Noor Niami

Don't Fall in Love

Why do you have to *fall* to be in love? You shouldn't have to fall for anyone or anything and love shouldn't make you fall; it should make you rise. So why is it that we always seem to fall in love? Can't we just be in love without falling? You can love someone without having to lose yourself, you can love someone but not at the expense of loving yourself less. Love needs to be balanced or else you'll end up loving the other person more than you love yourself and that's when things will begin to go downhill. When you lose yourself in the process of loving someone else you will begin to look at that person to fulfill you and meet all your needs. This person will then become the source to your well-being and happiness. Giving someone this immense power over you is extremely dangerous. Never give someone that amount of power over you, don't let someone else own you because you must own yourself. Don't give your power away to anyone so you don't fall. You can still love someone and hold yourself up high at the same time. Don't fall in the name of love, rise in love.

– Noor Niami

Lose it All to Gain it All

You need to lose everything at the start so you can gain yourself because once you've gained yourself you will gain it all. When you lose everything you fear losing, then you will have nothing else to fear. And if you have nothing left to lose, you now have everything left to gain. But in order to gain it all you must be willing to lose it all first and sometimes you need to lose what you thought you needed to gain everything you wanted. For everything we lose we gain something better. Be willing to lose it all knowing that you must lose everything in order to gain anything and the joy of regaining will exceed the pain of losing.

– Noor Niami

Burned Bridges

Some bridges will be burned so you can't cross them again. We have a tendency to go back to where we came from out of fear. We fear the unknown so we would rather go back to what we've once known then be dragged out of our comfort zone. But life will drag you out and force you to move from the place you've settled in. You were only supposed to pass by that place, not settle there and make it your home. You don't belong there and some bridges will be burned so you don't go back to the one thing you needed to get away from to save yourself. Sometimes you need to burn bridges to stop yourself from crossing them again and the bridges you burn will light the way forward.

– Noor Niami

Don't Be That Person

That person who goes back continuously and thinks that every time will be different. I know you miss them, and it's easier to live with them than to leave them. But isn't it easier to smile when they're not breaking your heart and hurting you with their actions? You don't deserve to be the backup plan. That person they drop and pick up whenever they feel like. Don't be that person. I have been there and I know what it's like to be disappointed by the same person time and time again. No one can tell you who to be, but don't be that person. You are smarter than that person, stronger than that person, and worth a lot more than being that person.

– Noor Niami

Patience is Key

Patience is the key to every door; patience and forbearance are the answers to every situation. When you master patience you master yourself, letting things unfold in their own timing. Learning patience is going to be difficult and hard to experience but once you conquer it you will find life easier. When you are patient you allow things to fall in the right place at the right time. Because you know that even when you get the right thing at the wrong time, it still makes it the wrong thing. Timing is everything and you cannot control how things unfold but you can control how you respond in the process of waiting, be sure to wait with a good attitude. God's plan takes time but the timing of it is perfect, it will take a little patience and a whole lot of faith but it's worth the wait. Don't go back for less just because you're impatient to wait for the best. Trust the process, your time is coming.

– Noor Niami

You Can't Fix Everything

Stop chasing after people and being the only one trying to fix everything. It's mentally, physically, and emotionally exhausting. You have to find peace with whoever comes and goes from your life. Don't be the only one putting in effort because you will lose yourself trying to save everyone else. Trust that whoever is meant to be there, will still be there.

– Noor Niami

Unbecoming Everything You're Not

Maybe it's not about becoming someone but unbecoming everything that you never were so you can return to your organic True Self. This is who you've always been but our inner traumatised parts have disconnected us from who we are. When you lovingly hold yourself and take yourself inwards to discover, embrace, and release the deeper beliefs and reasons that are holding you back from becoming who it is that you are called to be then you automatically go back to who you are truly meant to be. Maybe the journey isn't so much about becoming anything. Maybe it's about unbecoming everything that isn't you so you can be who you were meant to be in the first place.

– Noor Niami

My Silence

My silence speaks a thousand words, you're just not listening. My silence is just another form of communication for my pain. My silence means I am done with trying to teach you how to love me or treat me. My silence means I gave you my all and now I have nothing else to give. My silence means I am no longer worried about what will happen and just let it happen. My silence means I am done with trying to fix things that cannot fixed. My silence means I am letting go and trying to heal. And if you don't understand my silence then you will not understand my words.

– Noor Niami

Stop Playing Small

No one benefits from playing small and there is nothing empowering about shrinking yourself down for people to feel secure around you. We believe that we need to play small so that people won't feel insecure but their insecurity is for them to deal with not yours. It's time to stop hiding from the world and start stepping out with boldness. It's time to lead by example and not be led, it's time to speak up and share your voice, it's time to unleash your gifts and talents and stop hiding them. You were meant to stand out and shine so don't play small in fear of what other people might think of you. Give yourself permission to live a big life and step into the greatness of who you are meant to be.

– Noor Niami

It Just Wasn't Happening

I didn't lose you; I had to let you go.

I didn't get over you; I had to move on.

I didn't lose feelings for you; I had to walk away.

I didn't let you go; you pushed me away.

I didn't want things to end; I just did what's best for me.

I didn't want to break up; but I couldn't handle it anymore.

I didn't want to leave your life; but I just needed time to myself.

It's not that I didn't want to be with you because I did, but it's just that things weren't the same anymore. No matter how long I waited for things to get better, no matter how hard I tried to make things work, it just wasn't happening. It just got to the point where I put myself first for once because I didn't want to be unhappy anymore. I deserved to be happy even if meant away from you.

– Noor Niami

From Pain to Purpose

Don't be so afraid of pain; the pain is only there to teach you something and once you've learned the lesson your pain will leave you. It's just there to teach you something so let it do just that so it can leave you in peace. Most of the time, your purpose is revealed to you through your pain and the pain you're going through now will lead you to your purpose. You're not hurting for no reason; you're not suffering for no reason. Everything you're going through is happening for a very important reason. Your brokenness will create the platform for your calling. Don't let the pain cloud your vision because your pain will turn into your purpose.

– Noor Niami

I Walked Away

I walked away not because I didn't care, but because I was tired of giving you all the reasons why we should be together while you were giving me all the reasons why we can't be together. And no reason to stay is a good reason to go. You took my love and kindness for granted because you believed I was always going to be there. But I walked away; and not because I didn't care but because you didn't.

– Noor Niami

Shake The Dust From Your Feet

You'll go through places and people who don't accept you or welcome you into their lives. And the irony of all this is the more you try and get them to accept you, the more reasons you give them to reject you. But just because certain people don't welcome you it doesn't mean there aren't other people who will love and admire you. If they didn't accept you as their own then maybe you're not one of them. So shake the dust from your feet and move on. Maybe you're not meant to be where they are because you are going to better places. Maybe you're meant to be with better people who will love you and bring out the best in you. Maybe your life with them didn't work out because you are destined for a bigger life with better people. Don't lose hope and believe in fate, believe in your destiny, believe in your path because it will lead you to where you truly belong. Everything will work out for your best so bless those moments that broke your heart; they cracked you open so you could receive something better.

– Noor Niami

There is Nothing Wrong With You

When we're left with no choice but to let go of the one we love we start to wonder what is wrong with us. Why couldn't they just love us the way we loved them? Why wasn't I good enough? Something must be wrong with me. Sound familiar? I'm sure it does because we all do it. We all start asking these questions because we habitually start to equate our self-worth with their inability to see our worth and love us the way we want them to. But here's the thing; there is absolutely nothing wrong with you and if they couldn't love you the way you wanted to be loved then maybe they just weren't the right one for you. Because the right person who is meant for you will love you the way you deserve to be loved without having to show them or tell them how. And maybe you just needed to let go of the wrong person to find the right one.

– Noor Niami

Don't Take Them For Granted

When we're so consumed trying to make those whom we love, love us, we completely forget about the people who already do. Some people will love you only at your best and notice you when you shine but they're the same people who are not willing to accept you at your worst. They're not the ones who genuinely love you, they love who you are in that moment. But you are more than a moment and you will have good days and bad days. The people who are worthy of your love and care are not those who only accept you at your best but those who accept you at your worst. They are the ones who see you for who you are and accept you just the way you are. They don't need you to be different for them to love you, they just love you. They don't give excuses why they can't accept you and be there for you, because they just are. They love you, they accept you, they understand you, they see the best in you, they believe in you more than you believe in yourself. Don't take them for granted, they're the ones who deserve your love. Let go of those who only want you at your best because if they can't accept you at your worst then they surely don't deserve your best.

– Noor Niami

The Power of Your Words

Your words have power; every word you speak has the power to make or break, to heal or to hurt, to build or to destroy. They can crush a spirit or liberate it; they can break a heart or mend it. They shatter dreams or give hope, they can construct or destruct. So you need to choose your words wisely because once they are said they cannot be taken back. The tongue is a small thing but has enormous power, for death and life are in the power of the tongue. So be careful with your words because they are a living force and carry with them great power.

– Noor Niami

You Deserve to Know

You deserve to know; I loved you, I still do. You will forever have a part of my heart with you. After all this time, not a day goes by without you crossing my mind. Not a single day. Every day I remember you, every day I think about you, and every day I miss you. After everything we've been through, after all the pain and turmoil you put me in, my heart has never learned to hate you. Because the heart that loves you can never hate you.

– Noor Niami

Follow Your Soul

Follow your soul; it knows the way. Your soul never gets it wrong so learn to trust it more. No one knows your dreams and what you need to get there more than your soul. Only you know what you need in any moment so make sure you do just that. Life isn't easy and everyone is struggling one way or another. We all have a dream, a destination, and a goal to achieve and we all want to be somewhere. But only your soul knows what you need and how you'll get there. Your dream is personal to you and so is your journey. Don't compare yourself to others because their journey is different to yours, and don't follow someone else's way because your soul knows the best way. Follow your soul and trust your heart. Remember that you are not perfect; you are a work in progress, transforming daily into the masterpiece you were created to be.

– Noor Niami

You Are a Good Person

Don't repay them back with the same; don't give them a taste of their own medicine. Because you are better than that and you can do better than that. If they've hurt you, then you bless them anyway. If they've lied to you, you remain honest anyway. If they broke you, you remain strong anyway. If they disrespected you, you remain respectful anyway. Always stay true to yourself and don't be someone you're not. Don't let their poor actions change your character because your character is far more valuable than their behaviour. Be who you are and let others value and respect the person you are, not the person you're not. Never regret being a good person even to the wrong people. You are a good person; don't let a bad person change the goodness of who you are.

– Noor Niami

The Beauty of Pain

This is Your Healing

Even now, as broken as you may feel, you are still beautiful. Your pain doesn't change the beauty of who you are. As shattered as you may feel right now, you are still strong for holding yourself together and moving forward. Don't give up on yourself because you are worthy of fighting for. This is your healing, it doesn't have to make sense, and it doesn't have to be pretty. Let it be what it needs to be. You just have to hang in there and be sure to love yourself in the process. You deserve the love you give to others because you are far more worthy of that love than anyone else. One day you will tell your story of how you overcame what you went through and it will be a light in someone else's darkness.

– Noor Niami

You Can't Control the Uncontrollable

You can't control how other people respond to you because everything you say or do gets filtered through their lenses of whatever they have going on in that moment. Don't take it personal because it's not about you, it's about them and what they're going through. We have a tendency to control people and situations but we can't control the uncontrollable. The only person you can control is yourself and the only power you have is over yourself. No matter what anyone else is or isn't doing, keep doing your thing with love and integrity. You can't control people but you can control your reactions to them.

– Noor Niami

It's Not The End

The hardest thing you've ever had to do is to pull yourself out of a toxic situation with someone you love deeply. Sometimes the people you wanted as part of your story are only meant to be a chapter of your story, and coming to terms with that will be the hardest thing you do. Sometimes we hold on for far too long because we're not ready to let go and that's okay. Letting go of someone you love will be the hardest and dearest thing you have to let go of. But sooner or later you will need to close the chapter so your story can continue. Don't waste your time and energy on things you can't change. One bad chapter isn't the end of your story.

– Noor Niami

You Are Entitled to Your Feelings

Don't allow anyone to invalidate and minimise how you feel. If you feel something deeply then it's real to you and don't let anyone make you feel bad for feeling a certain way. They're not walking in your shoes; they're not living your story. They don't see life through your eyes and they don't dwell in your mind. They don't know the demons you are facing and no one else has lived through your experience. So no one has the power to invalidate how you feel and they certainly don't have the right to judge you for feeling the way you feel. Your feelings are important to you; they are real and deserve to be heard. Don't justify yourself for feeling a certain way and don't explain yourself to anyone because they haven't walked in your shoes and travelled your path. This is your journey, this is your battle, and everything you're going through is valid and your feelings matter. Don't let anyone make you believe otherwise.

– Noor Niami

You Can't Force Anything

In life I have learned you cannot force people to love you. If someone does not meet you where you are, you cannot keep asking them to do so. You cannot pour your love into a vessel that cannot contain it. You cannot pour your love into a soul not willing to receive it. You will only end up breaking yourself in the attempt to fix them. You have to walk away. When you learn you are worthy of love just the way you are, and deserve to be loved without having to beg for it, you open yourself up to a world of happiness and self-acceptance.

– Noor Niami

Dare to Dream

Dare to dream but most importantly dare to believe in your dreams no matter how big they may seem to you at the time. Your dream is for you to dream and for you to believe in and the only thing that will stop you from getting there is yourself. When you doubt and question yourself, your ability, and deservedness; that's when you hold yourself back from the very thing that is calling you. It's okay to not know how you're going to get there; rarely anyone does when they first begin. But you must start taking steps towards your dream no matter how big or small they are. Every small step in the right direction counts and it's your faith that will get you there. If you can believe it then you can achieve it. Don't be discouraged by failures, they only appear to redirect you to success and with every closed door a new one opens. Be at peace with yourself and with your journey because you cannot get to your destination when you are despising the journey. Believe in your dream and believe in yourself, learn from your mistakes and let your setbacks become a setup for your comeback. Believe you will get there and you will. So dare to dream and above all believe in your worthiness and deservedness to achieve your dream.

— Noor Niami

Enough is Enough

Seriously, at some point, you're going to have to be strong and say enough is enough. Take your stand, speak up, and refuse to let others hurt you by not giving them a place in your life. Throughout your lifetime some people will discredit you, disrespect you, and treat you poorly for no good reason at all. And even if there was a reason, it'll have nothing to do with you and everything to do with them. The only way some people can feel better about themselves is by putting others down. Don't consume yourself with trying to change them or win their approval. And don't make any space in your heart to hate them because the hate you consume will rob you of your peace. You cannot control what others think about you, but you do have control over how you internalize their opinions. Let them be and leave them to their own judgments. Let people love you for who you are and not for who they want you to be. Or let them walk away if they choose. They can't harm you either way; it's their understanding that is faulty, not yours.

– Noor Niami

You Are Not Alone

When you are going through something, when you are going through a rough time please remember that you are not alone. Every single person in this world has problems and struggles of their own. It doesn't matter who they are or what they have, no one is exempt from hard times. Just because someone might show you they're holding it together on the outside it doesn't mean that their inside isn't shattering into pieces. You too held it together on the outside when you were dying on the inside remember? Someone's outer life is by no means an indication of their inner life and those you may think are the happiest people on earth are actually the ones fighting bigger battles no one knows anything about. My point is; we are in this together, we all struggle, we all have our demons, and we all fight battles no one knows anything about. So you are anything but alone, our troubles may be different but we all have them and we all struggle with them the same. So don't look at others assuming they have it all together while you're losing it all because truth be told their problems could be bigger than yours and more hurtful than yours. And once you know you are not alone in this then you find rest and relief by knowing we are all in this together. Light will shine through your broken pieces, and grace and power will mend your heart.

– Noor Niami

Golden Glory

Let the struggles and hardship of life polish and shine you back into your golden glory. Everything has been working together to bring you back to unity. Each moment was participating in your return to God/Divine/Creator who has been present all along, within everyone and everything. Those who have hurt you the most have blessed you the greatest, raising to the surface all pain, suffering, and hardship that already lay within. In truth, they did not cause anything they merely echoed in resonance something that was there since the beginning of time. That which had to go, needed to be dissolved, and was to be released. They did not destroy you; they have reconstructed you and they have not blocked you; they have set you free. The question is;

Will *you* set yourself free?

– Noor Niami

The Beauty of Pain

"Strength doesn't reside in never having been broken but in the courage to grow strong in the broken places."

Kristen Jongen

About the Author

Noor Niami is an Iraqi-Australian author, speaker, and creator; but above all, she is a woman of God. Her passion to help others has become her purpose in life. She is determined to empower those who have been hurt, heartbroken, and mistreated, by sharing her personal experiences and revelations. Coming from a place of brokenness herself she knows what it feels like to be in that dark place desperately waiting to see the light at the end of the tunnel. It wasn't until she refused to wait any longer and decided to become the light she needed instead, and wants everybody to do the same. She urges everyone to heal themselves back to wholeness, raise their voices, rise up, and soar.

For more information visit:
www.noorniami.com

CPSIA information can be obtained
at www.ICGtesting.com
Printed in the USA
BVHW081620240920
589462BV00002B/106